JAMES ANDRACHUCK, CHRIS BOLDT, STELLA CHEUNG BOYLAND, OLYVIA BUANA, BRUCE CARSCADDEN, EMMA CARSCADDEN, JASON CHU, PEARL CHUANG, JILLIAN COCHRANE, ALAN DAVIES, ANGELA ENMAN, SAL GALLAGHER, BRITT GALLPEN, TANGIE GENSHOREK, CARSTEN GOEHLER, MATT HALVERSON, LARRAINE HENNING, MELISSA HIGGS, LISA KWAN, LEA LEDOHOWSKI, YVONNE LEUNG, ARMEN MAMOURIAN, RYAN MCCUAIG, IAN ROSS MCDONALD, KURT MCLAREN, PETER MCRAE, SCOTT MITCHELL, KEITH NG, JOHN RODDICK, KRISTINA SEO, AYME SHARMA, GLEN STOKES, TINA TAJITSU BOLDT, TERRY TREMAYNE, KATHERINE WOOD.

CARSCADDEN **THRIFT**

SELECTED PROJECTS

With an essay by Jim Nicholls

First published in 2011 by BLUE*IM*PRINT www.readleaf.ca
Content © 2011 the Contributors

CIP Data available from Library and Archives Canada Cataloguing in Publication

ISBN: 978-1-897476-40-6

We gratefully acknowledge for their financial support of our publishing program the Canada Council for the Arts, the BC Arts Council, and the Government of Canada through the Book Publishing Industry Development Program (BPIDP).

Author Bruce Carscadden Architect (Firm)
Editor Ian Ross McDonald MAIBC
Texts Jim Nichols, Ian Ross McDonald MAIBC
Photos Bruce Carscadden Architect (Firm); Digital Perfections: 9, 11, 23-27, 35-39, 50, 72, 74, 80, 88, 92, 94; Martin Knowles Photo Media: 29-33, 41-45, 82, 84, 86, 96, 106-110.
Design Ian Ross McDonald MAIBC

10 9 8 7 6 5 4 3 2 1

Printed in Singapore

CONTENTS

	PHOTOGRAPHS	DRAWINGS
Public Architects, by Jim Nicholls		
Swalwell Park, Kensington Park & Robert Burnaby Park Washrooms	8	46
Terrace Arena	18	66
Winfield Arena Dressing Rooms	22	72
Renfrew Community Centre Renovations	28	82
Penticton Aquatic Centre	34	88
Private Residence	40	96
On Thrift, by Ian Ross McDonald		106
Projects & Awards		107

PUBLIC ARCHITECTS

Bruce Carscadden is the founding principal of the eponymous architectural firm, Bruce Carscadden Architect in Vancouver BC. Currently with one partner, Glen Stokes, an associate, and eight other architects, interns, and assistants, the studio has been producing projects throughout British Columbia and across Canada for just over ten years. Their portfolio of work includes a broad range of institutional and commercial work, historical loft conversions, and significant residential commissions, but it is defined and distinguished by an eloquent body of public architecture. Aquatic centers, community and civic buildings, and municipal park amenities demonstrate an accomplished professional passion for the tectonics and material details of architecture, a humane engagement with a diverse public, and a refined, pragmatic utility, tempered with an engaging wit.

Telling Details
With challenging programs that require careful consideration of matter-of-fact necessities and which operate within tightly defined budgets, the work of the firm emphatically manifests an ability to transform constraint into opportunity. Bruce Carscadden Architect mines inherent characteristics of material, program and site for their expressive potentials, where the given problem is turned into the telling details of a desirable solution. In several recent projects, BCA floats a horizontal surface of solid phenolic free of painted block walls, replacing the difficult junction of countertop to backsplash with a modest modernist reveal, that also reduces the need for perpetual maintenance. In other projects, the firm alters expectations for standard structural concrete block, a sufficiently robust material for intensively used facilities, with subtle shifts that create the variegated relief of a textile wall, or with intermittent gaps between blocks that allow the wall to breath and transmit light. For the Renfrew Park Community Centre

(Vancouver BC, 2010) BCA convinced a conservative client to turn ubiquitous change room lockers into a refined aesthetic asset. On a research tour of swimming pools in Germany, Carscadden identified a Swiss-made locker with colored opaque glass doors, and arranged their first-time import to Canada through a British distributor, installing them in Renfrew Park, completely transforming the feel of the change room.

Social Terrains
The firm successfully works to encourage and nurture the potential opportunities for human engagement inherent in the demanding programs of public buildings. They deftly and economically insert meaningful social terrains within the original mandate of client requirements, while adding value to the initial scope with considered details that allow required building elements to perform double duty. In a clear illustration of this generosity of form, BCA often creates places for the public to sit and gather, not just with the requisite bench, but also with the thoughtful shaping of the concrete groundwork at column bases, retaining walls, and stairs. In an early example of this, robust columns supporting the floating roof of the Grandview Outdoor Classroom (Vancouver BC, 1999-2000) meet the earth with a swelling and stepping of their concrete base, articulating both grounded stability and sheltered seating. At the Robert Burnaby Park Washrooms (Burnaby BC, 2008) a facility embedded in the slope of a hill, an adjacent retaining wall carves out an informal amphitheater, a durable and encouraging location for local youth to meet. The stairs to the entry of the Winfield Arena (Lake Country BC, 2010) which face the morning sun, parking, and a drive-by drop off, slide past the handrail and double up to provide a cascading plinth of available seating as people wait for a ride, or pause together on the porch.

Human Factors

The primary beneficiaries of the firm's work are not only informed architectural observers, but also an inclusive and broad spectrum of the general public. The ideas embedded in the projects are accessible and legible, but not overly didactic. BCA often deploys a playful or humanizing touch as a sophisticated strategy aimed at creating an empathetic connection between architect, artifact, and audience. As an illustrative case, the gender identification of change room and washroom doors manifest a witty, poetic engagement with the authentic materiality of the project: set into the board-formed concrete wall of the Robert Burnaby Park Washrooms fossilized male and female figures call out the washroom doors. At the Swalwell Park Washrooms (Lake Country BC, 2008) door identification signs made with perforated, galvanized steel screens, allow the passage of filtered light and air to illustrate and enliven the entry. Holes of varying sizes create the pixilated image of a man and woman: friendly sentries standing by their respective doors. Round, head-sized, glowing white lights illuminate the change room entries at the Renfrew Park Community Centre: they act as both fixture and face of the life-sized identifying figure painted on the concrete block wall. By calling out additional change room and washroom doors with the figures of a man and woman holding the hands of a child, BCA has led pioneering efforts to redefine the public program with family oriented facilities.

Expressive Restraint
The work of Bruce Carscadden Architect represents the focused effort of a firm of publicly engaged architects. It exhibits a sympathetic and enlightened attitude towards the unique constraints and opportunities of building in the public realm. Together, the firm meets the rigorous demands of economy with a luxury of sprit and inventiveness, exercising artful intelligence to humanize necessity, and to find fun in function, all the while producing solutions in which less is not only more, but enough.

Jim Nicholls
University of Washington
College of Built Environments
Department of Architecture
October 30, 2010

SWALWELL PARK, KENSINGTON PARK & ROBERT BURNABY PARK WASHROOMS

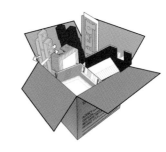

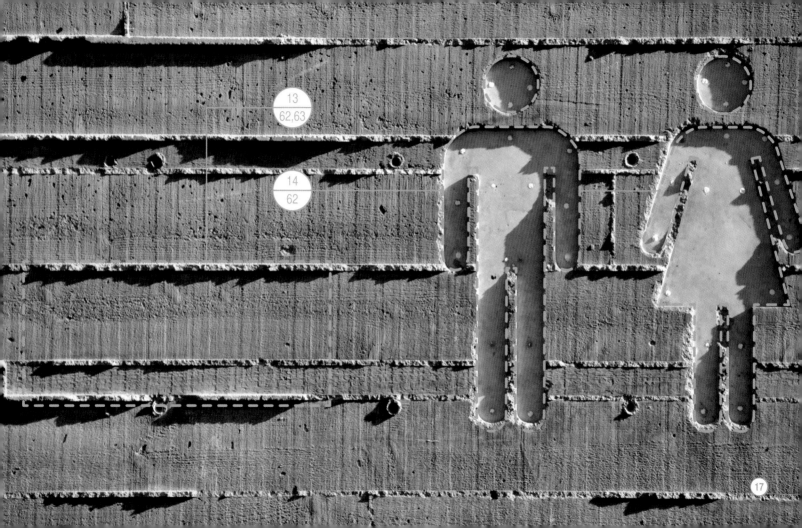

TERRACE ARENA

67

15
69

16
67,69

17
68,69

21

WINFIELD ARENA DRESSING ROOMS

A'   Z

10'-0"

MIN. DIST. REQ. FOR 2
PLAYERS WHO FOUGHT
LAST WEEK TO PASS EACH
OTHER WITHOUT INCIDENT

CORRIDOR
323

18
75

19
79

22
76

25
75,77

26
81

27

RENFREW COMMUNITY CENTRE RENOVATIONS

Phasing

User Group Demandds

Achitectural Ambitions

Hazardous Materials

Client Operational Requirements

Health Code Upgrades

Tight Money

28
86

29
83

30
86

31

0.95m

83

33

PENTICTON AQUATIC CENTRE

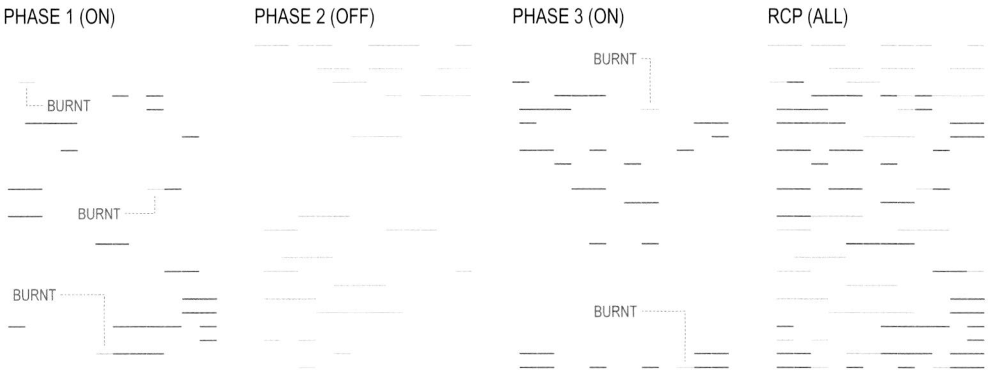

PHASE 1 (ON)

BURNT

BURNT

BURNT

PHASE 2 (OFF)

PHASE 3 (ON)

BURNT

BURNT

RCP (ALL)

EXIT

fitness

35
90

SWIM CL MEETING ROOM DOMIN

PRIVATE RESIDENCE

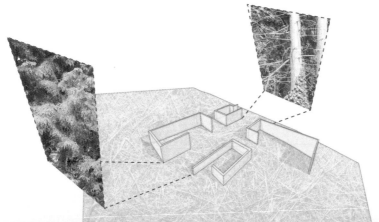

37
99

38
100

39
100

40
100,103

41
103

42
102

43
104

44
105

SWALWELL PARK WASHROOM

CLIENT   The District of Lake Country
DESIGN TEAM   Bruce Carscadden Architect, CWMM Consulting Engineers, Jade West Engineering, Falcon Engineering, Catherine Berris & Associates
CONTRACTORS   Forma Construction (Washroom), Tri-City Contracting (Pavilion)

PHASE 1: WASHROOMS

LOT A
PLAN KAP45331

PHASE 2: PAVILION

CREEK

WATER PARK (BY OTHERS)

Bottom Wood Lake Road

270°54'44"   270°54'44"
13.26   66.978

GATE   GATE
POST   POST

EXISTING MONUMENT
APPROX. PROPOSED SANITARY (SEE CIVIL)
APPROX. PROPOSED WATER
(SEE CIVIL AND ALTERNATE PRICE #1)
EXISTING ASPHALT DRIVE/PATCH & REPAIR

1 STOREY MASONRY WASHROOM
BUILDING SHOWN TONED

EXISTING GRAVEL
PARKING AREA

SKATEBOARD
PARK

270°00'00"
131.560

BACKSTOP

GOALPOSTS

DENOTES PROPERTY LINE

EXISTING STORAGE/GARAGE

TREE PROTECTION BARRIER
3.6m FROM TREE; MINIMUM 1.2m HIGH
CONSTRUCTED OF SNOW FENCING OR
PLYWOOD NAILED TO WOOD STAKES.

APPROXIMATE CONTRACT AREA;
RESERVED CONTRACTOR PARKING
TO CONSIST OF 6 PARKING SPACES
IN EXISTING PARKING LOT.

FUTURE AND MASTERPLAN
SHOWN IN GREY

EXISTING
PIT TOILET

LOT B
PLAN KAP45331

FIELD

GENERAL NOTES

1
SITE PLAN INFORMATION TAKEN FROM RUSSELL N.
SHORTT "PLAN SHOWING BUILDING ON SITE PLAN
OF PARK" (FEBRUARY 2005)
2
ALL DIMENSIONS OF THE EXISTING BUILDINGS AND
STRUCTURES TO BE CONFIRMED ON SITE
3
PROPOSED GRID LINES ARE LOCATED AT THE
OUTSIDE FACE OF CONCRETE WALLS TYPICAL
4
CIVIL WORK 3' BEYOND THE BOUNDARY OF THE
BUILDING IS ILLUSTRATED HERE FOR
COORDINATION.
5
LEGAL DESCRIPTION AS INDICATED ON SURVEY:
LOTS A & B, PLAN KAP45331, D.L., 118,
O.D.Y..D, WINFIELD, BC

FENCE

GOALPOSTS   GATE

FENCE
258.000

EDGE OF DRIVEWAY

BACKSTOP   FENCE

Bottom Wood Lake Road

1 SITE PLAN
1:400

bruce carscadden ARCHITECT inc

8250 - 45 Dunlevy Avenue
Vancouver BC V6A 3A3
604.633.1800 phone
604.633.1800 fax
office@carscadden-architect.com

TENDER   27 JUNE 2007
ISSUE   DATE
Revisions

Job Title
SWALWELL PARK
BUILDING

Sheet Title
SITE PLAN

Drawn   irm
Checked   BC
Job No   06-20
Date   27 JUNE 2007
Scale   1:400 METRIC

Sheet
A2
47

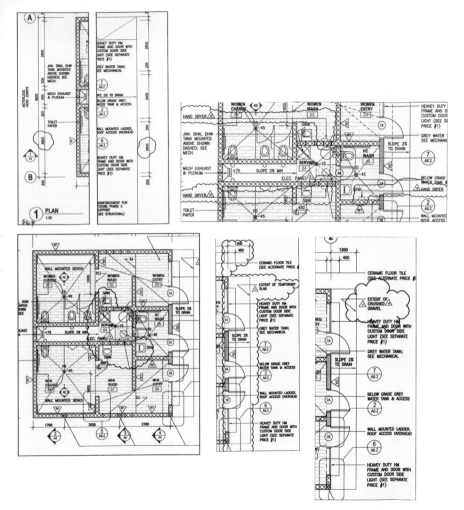

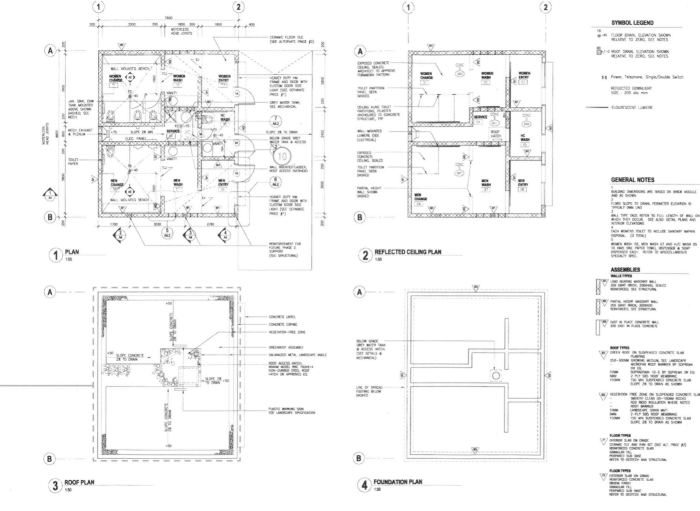

8280 - 45 Dunlevy Avenue
Vancouver BC V6A 3A3
604.633.1800 phone
604.633.1809 fax
office@carscadden-architect.com

bruce carscadden **ARCHITECT** inc

SYMBOL LEGEND

FD/-45 FLOOR DRAIN, ELEVATION SHOWN
RELATIVE TO ZERO, SEE NOTES

RD/-0 ROOF DRAIN, ELEVATION SHOWN
RELATIVE TO ZERO, SEE NOTES

$S Power, Telephone, Single/Double Switch

REFLECTED DOWNLIGHT
SIZE : 200 dia mm

FLOURESCENT LUMIERE

GENERAL NOTES

1
BUILDING DIMENSIONS ARE BASED ON BRICK MODULE
AND AS SHOWN
2
FLOORS SLOPE TO DRAIN, PERIMETER ELEVATION IS
TYPICALLY 0MM U/NO
3
WALL TYPE TAGS REFER TO FULL LENGTH OF WALL ON
WHICH THEY OCCUR. SEE ALSO: DETAIL PLANS AND
INTERIOR ELEVATIONS
4
EACH WOMENS TOILET TO INCLUDE SANITARY NAPKIN
DISPOSAL. (3 TOTAL)
5
WOMEN WASH 02, MEN WASH 07 AND H/C WASH 05
TO HAVE ONE PAPER TOWEL DISPENSER & SOAP
DISPENSER EACH. REFER TO MISCELLANEOUS
SPECIALTY SPEC.

ASSEMBLIES

WALLS TYPES

W1 LOAD BEARING MASONRY WALL
200 GIANT BRICK, 200X400, SEALED
REINFORCED, SEE STRUCTURAL

W2 PARTIAL HEIGHT MASONRY WALL
200 GIANT BRICK, 200X400
REINFORCED, SEE STRUCTURAL

W3 CAST IN PLACE CONCRETE WALL
200 CAST IN PLACE CONCRETE

ROOF TYPES

R1 GREEN ROOF ON SUSPENDED CONCRETE SLAB
PLANTING
250-300MM GROWING MEDIUM, SEE LANDSCAPE
MICROFAB ROOT BARRIER BY SOPREMA
OR EQ.
10MM SOPRADRAIN 10-G BY SOPREMA OR EQ.
6MM 2 PLY SBS ROOF MEMBRANE
150MM 150 MIN SUSPENDED CONCRETE SLAB
SLOPE 2% TO DRAIN AS SHOWN

R2 VEGETATION FREE ZONE ON SUSPENDED CONCRETE SLAB
SMOOTH FINISH 50-100MM ROCKS
R20 RIGID INSULATION WHERE NOTED
ROOT BARRIER
10MM LANDSCAPE DRAIN MAT
6MM 2-PLY SBS ROOF MEMBRANE
150MM 150 MIN SUSPENDED CONCRETE SLAB
SLOPE 2% TO DRAIN AS SHOWN

FLOOR TYPES

F1 INTERIOR SLAB ON GRADE
CERAMIC TILE AND PAN SET (SEE ALT. PRICE #2)
REINFORCED CONCRETE SLAB
PREPARED SUB BASE
REFER TO GEOTECH AND STRUCTURAL

FLOOR TYPES

F2 EXTERIOR SLAB ON GRADE
REINFORCED CONCRETE SLAB
BROOM FINISH
GRANULAR FILL
PREPARED SUB BASE
REFER TO GEOTECH AND STRUCTURAL

TENDER 27 JUNE 2007
ISSUE DATE
Revision

JOB TITLE

SWALWELL PARK
BUILDING

N

SHEET TITLE

PLANS

Drawn crm
Checked BC
Job No 08-20
Date 27 JUNE 2007
Scale 1:50 METRIC

A3
49

---

1 **PLAN** 1:50

2 **REFLECTED CEILING PLAN** 1:50

3 **ROOF PLAN** 1:50

4 **FOUNDATION PLAN** 1:50

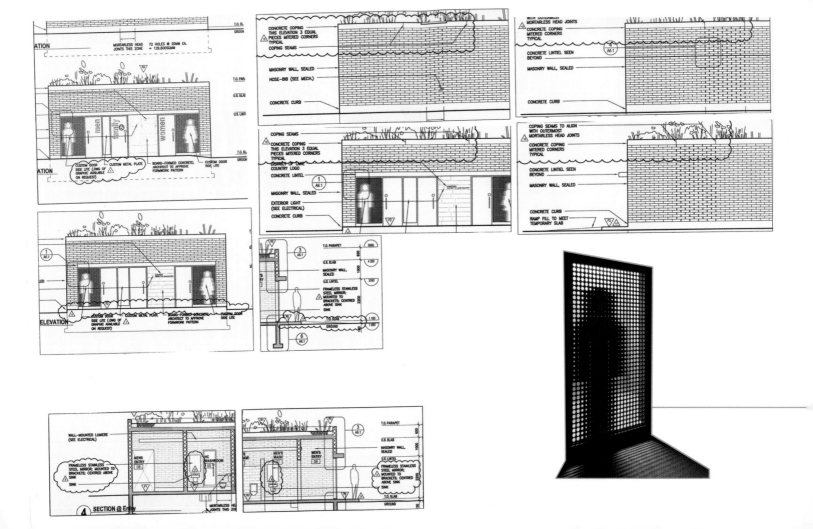

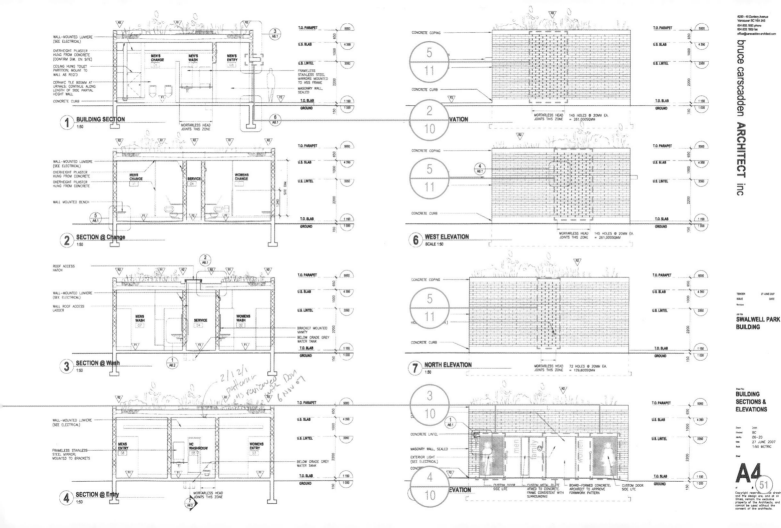

6280 - 40 Dunlevy Avenue
Vancouver BC V6A 3A3
604.633.1830 phone
604.633.1820 fax
office@carscadden-architect.com

bruce carscadden ARCHITECT inc

1 BUILDING SECTION 1:50

WALL-MOUNTED LUMIERE (SEE ELECTRICAL)
OVERHEIGHT PLASTER HUNG FROM CONCRETE (CONFIRM DIM. ON SITE)
CEILING HUNG TOILET PARTITION; MOUNT TO WALL AS REQ'D
CERAMIC TILE 800MM AT URINALS; CONTINUE ALONG LENGTH OF SIDE PARTIAL HEIGHT WALL
CONCRETE CURB

MEN'S CHANGE — MEN'S WASH — MEN'S ENTRY

FRAMELESS STAINLESS STEEL MIRRORS MOUNTED TO HSS FRAME
MASONRY WALL, SEALED

T.O. PARAPET 5000 · U.S. SLAB 4350 · U.S. LINTEL 3350 · 2200 · T.O. SLAB 1150 · GROUND 1000

MORTARLESS HEAD JOINTS THIS ZONE

2 SECTION @ Change 1:50

WALL-MOUNTED LUMIERE (SEE ELECTRICAL)
OVERHEIGHT PLASTER HUNG FROM CONCRETE
OVERHEIGHT PLASTER HUNG FROM CONCRETE
WALL MOUNTED BENCH

MEN'S CHANGE — SERVICE — WOMENS CHANGE

3 SECTION @ Wash 1:50

ROOF ACCESS HATCH
WALL-MOUNTED LUMIERE (SEE ELECTRICAL)
WALL ROOF ACCESS LADDER

MENS WASH — SERVICE — WOMENS WASH

BRACKET MOUNTED VANITY
BELOW GRADE GREY WATER TANK

4 SECTION @ Entry 1:50

WALL-MOUNTED LUMIERE (SEE ELECTRICAL)
FRAMELESS STAINLESS STEEL MIRROR; MOUNTED TO BRACKETS

MENS ENTRY — HC WASHROOM — WOMENS ENTRY

BELOW GRADE GREY WATER TANK
MORTARLESS HEAD JOINTS THIS ZONE

2/12/1
Buttcross
4's removed...
level Don
6 Nov 07

2 ELEVATION 1:50

CONCRETE COPING
CONCRETE CURB
MORTARLESS HEAD JOINTS THIS ZONE   146 HOLES @ 20MM EA. = 261,000SQMM

6 WEST ELEVATION SCALE 1:50

CONCRETE COPING
CONCRETE CURB
MORTARLESS HEAD JOINTS THIS ZONE   145 HOLES @ 20MM EA. = 261,000SQMM

7 NORTH ELEVATION 1:50

CONCRETE COPING
CONCRETE CURB
MORTARLESS HEAD JOINTS THIS ZONE   72 HOLES @ 20MM EA. = 129,600SQMM

ELEVATION 1:50

CONCRETE LINTEL
MASONRY WALL, SEALED
EXTERIOR LIGHT (SEE ELECTRICAL)
CONCRETE

men   family   women

CUSTOM DOOR SIDE LITE   CUSTOM METAL PLATE AFFIXED TO CONCRETE FRAME CONSISTENT WITH SURROUNDING   BOARD-FORMED CONCRETE; ARCHITECT TO APPROVE FORMWORK PATTERN   CUSTOM DOOR SIDE LITE

TENDER   27 JUNE 2007
ISSUE   06-20
Revisions

Job Title
SWALWELL PARK
BUILDING

Sheet Title
BUILDING
SECTIONS &
ELEVATIONS

Drawn   imn
Checked   BC
Job No.   06-20
Date   27 JUNE 2007
Scale   1:50 METRIC

Sheet

A4
51

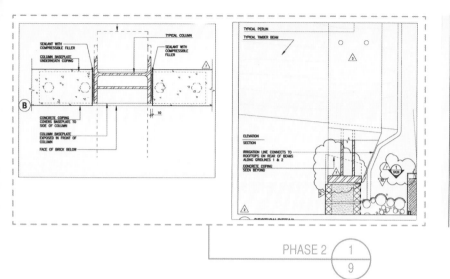

Detail B (Column/Coping)
- SEALANT WITH COMPRESSIBLE FILLER
- COLUMN BASEPLATE UNDERNEATH COPING
- TYPICAL COLUMN
- SEALANT WITH COMPRESSIBLE FILLER
- B
- CONCRETE COPING COVERS BASEPLATE TO SIDE OF COLUMN
- COLUMN BASEPLATE EXPOSED IN FRONT OF COLUMN
- FACE OF BRICK BELOW
- 10

Section Detail
- TYPICAL PERLIN
- TYPICAL TIMBER BEAM
- ELEVATION
- SECTION
- IRRIGATION LINE CONNECTS TO ROOFTOPS ON REAR OF BEAMS ALONG GRIDLINES 1 & 2
- CONCRETE COPING SEEN BEYOND
- SIGN
- SECTION DETAIL

PHASE 2 (1/9)

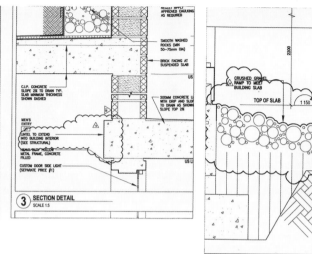

Section Detail 3 (SCALE 1:5)
- APPLY APPROVED CAULKING AS REQUIRED
- SMOOTH WASHED ROCKS (MIN 50–75mm DIA)
- BRICK FACING AT SUSPENDED SLAB
- C.I.P. CONCRETE SLOPE 2% TO DRAIN TYP. SLAB MINIMUM THICKNESS SHOWN DASHED
- 200mm CONCRETE L WITH DRIP AND SLO TO DRAIN AS SHOWN SLOPE TOP 2%
- MEN'S ENTRY
- LINTEL TO EXTEND INTO BUILDING INTERIOR (SEE STRUCTURAL)
- HEAVY-DUTY HOLLOW METAL FRAME, CONCRETE FILLED
- CUSTOM DOOR SIDE LIGHT (SEPARATE PRICE #1)
- US L
- 3 SECTION DETAIL SCALE 1:5

Top of Slab Detail
- 2200
- CRUSHED GRAVEL RAMP TO MEET BUILDING SLAB
- TOP OF SLAB
- 1 150

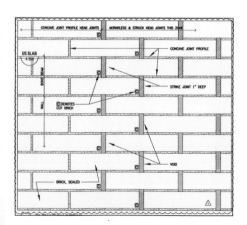

Brick Coursing Detail
- CONCAVE JOINT PROFILE HEAD JOINTS
- NORMAL/ESS & STRUCK HEAD JOINTS THIS ZONE
- US SLAB
- CONCAVE JOINT PROFILE
- STRIKE JOINT 1" DEEP
- DENOTES CUT BRICK
- VOID
- BRICK, SEALED

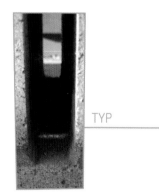

TYP

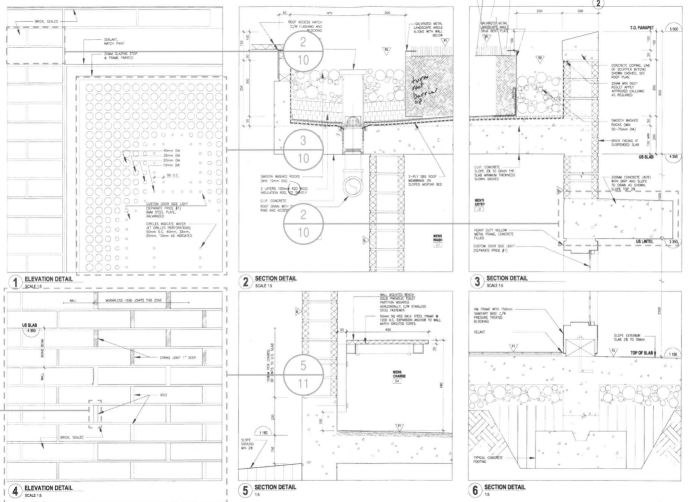

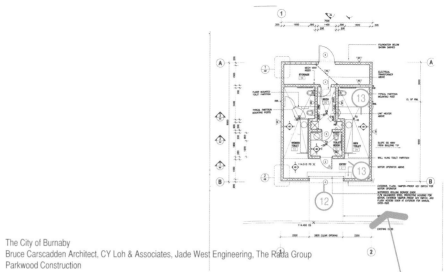

KENSINGTON PARK WASHROOM

CLIENT	The City of Burnaby
DESIGN TEAM	Bruce Carscadden Architect, CY Loh & Associates, Jade West Engineering, The Rada Group
CONTRACTORS	Parkwood Construction

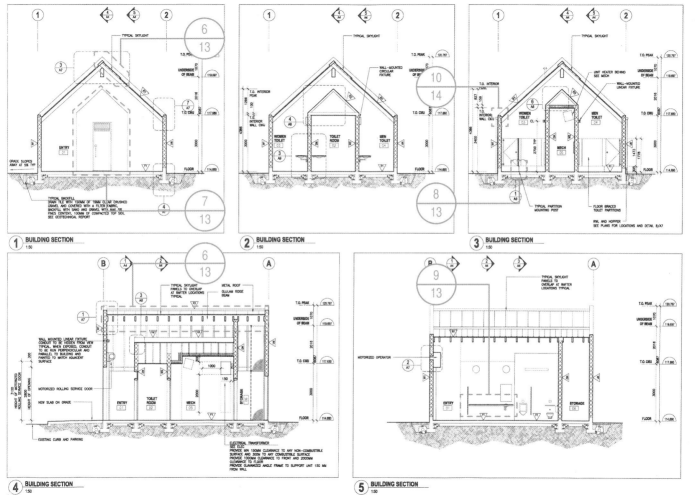

#250 - 45 Dunlevy Avenue
Vancouver BC V6A 3A3
604.633.1830 phone
604.633.1809 fax
office@carscadden-architect.com

bruce carscadden ARCHITECT inc

1 BUILDING SECTION
1:50

2 BUILDING SECTION
1:50

3 BUILDING SECTION
1:50

4 BUILDING SECTION
1:50

5 BUILDING SECTION
1:50

ISSUED FOR CONST.   FEB 11, 2008
ISSUED FOR DP   NOV 26, 2007
ISSUED FOR TENDER   NOV 21, 2007
ISSUED FOR DP   OCT 31, 2007
ISSUED FOR COSTING   OCT 19, 2007

KENSINGTON
PARK BUILDING

BUILDING
SECTIONS

Drawn   CS
Checked   BC
Job No.   07-14
Date   AUG 2007
Scale   1:50

A4
55

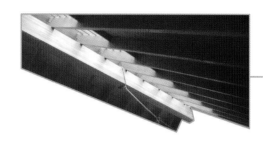

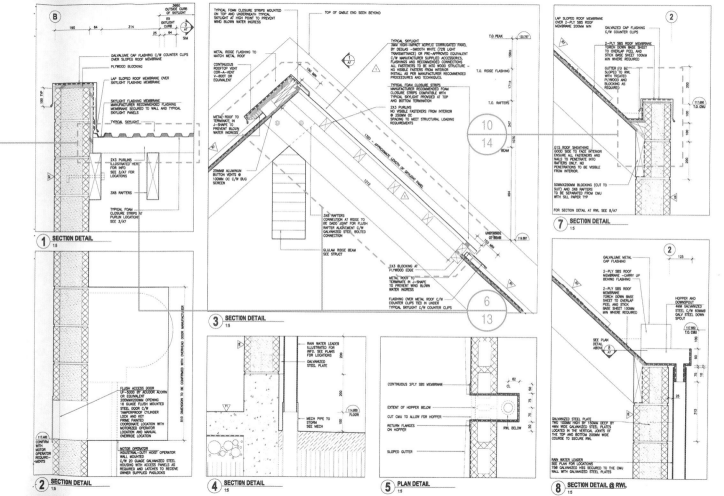

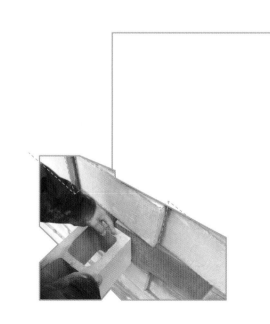

#202 - 48 Dunlevy Avenue
Vancouver BC V6A 3A3
604.633.1830 phone
604.633.1809 fax
office@carscadden-architect.com

bruce carscadden ARCHITECT inc

ISSUED FOR DP   NOV 08, 2007
ISSUED FOR TENDER NOV 01, 2007
ISSUED FOR COSTING OCT 19, 2007

Revisions

**KENSINGTON
PARK BUILDING**

DETAILS

Drawn	QS
Checked	BC
Job No	07-14
Date	AUG 2007
Scale	1:5

A8

59

1 PLAN DETAIL 1:5

190
17 TYP BLOCK MODULE 17

TYPICAL CMU
RUNNING BOND
GROUT SOLID
SEE STRUCT
ORTHOGONAL TO
GRID LINES
REFER TO
ELEVATIONS FOR
EXTENT

TYPICAL ROTATED CMU
ROTATE 5°
RUNNING BOND
DOUBLE-ENDERS ONLY
GROUT SOLID
SEE STRUCT
EACH SUCCESSIVE COURSE
TO BE ROTATED IN
OPPOSITE DIRECTION
ALIGN CL OF TYPICAL
ROTATED CMU TO CL OF
TYPICAL CMU
ENSURE EXPOSED
HORIZONTAL SURFACES ARE
FREE OF GROUT
REFER TO ELEVATIONS FOR
EXTENT

TYPICAL ROTATED
CMU SPACING

2 PLAN DETAIL 1:5

TYPICAL ROTATED
CMU SPACING

TYPICAL ROTATED CMU

TYPICAL CMU

TYPICAL CMU

190
17 TYP BLOCK MODULE 17

OUTER EXTENT OF
TYPICAL ROTATED BLOCK

3 SECTION DETAIL 1:5

HOLES IN PLYWOOD AS REQUIRED TO
PROVIDE ACCESS TO ANCHOR BOLTS

25MM WIDE
EDGING TO SUIT

TOP OF CMU WALL
CUT TO MATCH
SLOPE OF ROOF

2X6 SILL PLATE
C/W ANCHOR
BOLT - SEE
STRUCT

G1S PLYWOOD

2X6 STRUCTURE

4 SECTION DETAIL 1:5

11
15

ALUMINUM BUTTON
@ 100MM OC C/W
SCREEN
ATE ON WOMENS TOILET
SIDE OF PEAK ONLY

T.O. INTERIOR
PEAK

G1S PLYWOOD

2X8 STRUCTURE

ROOF SLOPE FLUSH
AND CONTINUOUS
C/W DETAIL 5/A8

25MM WIDE
EDGING TO
SUIT

LINE OF TOP OF CMU AT
GABLE END

2
A8

T.O. INTERIOR
CMU WALL

600

2 LAYERS OF 12MM
PLYWOOD. BOTTOM LAYER
IS G1S FACING DOWN

2X8 SILL PLATE
C/W ANCHOR
BOLT - SEE
STRUCT

CEILING GRILLE
600MM X 600MM SQUARE GRILLE
25MMX25MM PAINTED GALVANIZED
ANGLE FRAME TO PROTECT EXPOSED
EDGES OF PLYWOOD C/W
1-1/2"-#9 EXPANDED METAL MESH,
FLAT, PLAIN STEEL GRILLE - PT
GRILLE TO BE LOCATED BETWEEN
WOOD STRUCTURE ABOVE

WOMEN
TOILET
03

TOILET
ROOM
02

6 SECTION DETAIL 1:5

25MM∅ VENT HOLES
@ 100MM OC C/W
CONTINUOUS BUG SCREEN
ON UNDERSIDE OF PLYWOOD
LOCATE ON WOMENS TOILET
03 SIDE OF PEAK ONLY

MEN
TOILET
04

T.O. INTERIOR
PEAK

ROOF SLOPE FLUSH
AND CONTINUOUS
WITH DETAIL 3/A8

G1S PLYWOOD

2X8 STRUCTURE

25MM WIDE
EDGING TO
SUIT

T.O. INTERIOR
CMU WALL

WOMEN
TOILET
03

2X6 SILL PLATE
C/W ANCHOR
BOLT - SEE
STRUCT

MECH
05

ROBERT BURNABY PARK WASHROOM

CLIENT The City of Burnaby
DESIGN TEAM Bruce Carscadden Architect, CY Loh & Associates, Jade West Engineering, The Rada Group
CONTRACTOR Rogad Construction

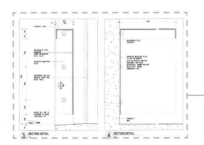

bruce carscadden ARCHITECT inc

#280 - 45 Dunlevy Avenue
Vancouver BC V6A 3A3
604.633.1800 phone
604.633.1805 fax
office@carscadden-architect.com

FLOOR PLAN (1)

200 · 2400 · 2800 · 2400 · 1800 · 200
10000
200 · 2400 · 200
200 · 1800 · 200

PC3

NEW ASPHALT
C/W TOPPING COURSE ON
150MM ROAD MULCH BASE
(19MM MINUS)
GEOTECHNICAL ENGINEER
REVIEW SUB-BASE
CONDITIONS PRIOR TO
APPLICATION OF ASPHALT

EXISTING ASPHALT

STEPPED
CONCRETE WALL

TYPICAL HANDRAIL
REFER TO DETAIL 5/A7

92.001 EG

PC3

MOTORIZED ROLLING SERVICE DOOR
C/W GALVANIZED STEEL PROTECTIVE HOUSING FOR MOTOR,
EXTERIOR TAMPER-PROOF KEY SWITCH, AND FLUSH ACCESS
DOOR AT EXTERIOR FOR MANUAL OVER-RIDE

91.968 EG
93.198 EG
92.015 DG
93.112 EG
92.015 DG

93.358 EG
92.209 DG
92.225 FG

91.945 DG   91.925 EG   91.952 EG

2% SLOPE
2% SLOPE

PC3

EXISTING GRAVEL
EXISTING ASPHALT

SEE ELEVATION FOR SITE
SECTION INFORMATION

ENTRY
MOTOR OPERATOR ABOVE
SEE DETAIL 8/A7
CONCESSION

MOTORIZED
ROLLING SERVICE
DOOR

GALVANIZED
STEEL
COUNTER

HIGH PRIVACY
TOILET PARTITION
FLOOR MOUNTED
AND OVERHEAD
BRACED.
OVERHEAD BRACE
TO BE GALVANIZED
25X50 HSS.
ALL TOILET
PARTITION DOORS
TO BE SET AS
CLOSED TYP

WOMEN
TOILET
13

TOILET
ROOM
12

MEN
TOILET
14

TYPICAL
PARTITION
MOUNTING POST
(SEVEN TOTAL)

MECH/ELEC
16

CONCESSION COUNTER
SIM TO DETAILS 2&3/A8
GALVANIZED HSS FRAME
TO HAVE FOUR ANGLE
SUPPORTS FOR COUNTER
SEE MECH FOR LAV
SPEC

UNIT HEATER
ABOVE

92.140 DG   2% SLOPE

SHAFT AND JUNCTION
DUCT ABOVE

VENT FROM ABOVE

LOCATE EXISTING LOCK-BLOCKS AS REQUIRED TO ABUT BUILDING
AND RETAIN EXISTING SLOPES.

EXCAVATION AND REINSTALLED. EXISTING CHAIN LINK FENCE TO
BE REINSTATED TO MATCH EXISTING, PATCH AND MAKE GOOD.

SEE ELEVATION FOR SITE
SECTION INFORMATION

GENERAL NOTES

1
BUILDING DIMENSIONS ARE BASED ON BRICK MODULE
AND AS SHOWN
2
FLOORS SLOPE TO DRAIN, PERIMETER ELEVATION IS
TYPICALLY 0MM UNO
3
WALL TYPE TAGS REFER TO FULL LENGTH OF WALL ON
WHICH THEY OCCUR UNLESS NOTED OTHERWISE.
SEE ALSO: DETAIL PLANS AND INTERIOR ELEVATIONS

EXISTING "LOCK-BLOCK" WALL

EXISTING CHAIN LINK FENCE

WASHROOM ACCESSORIES

1
EVERY TOILET TO INCLUDE ONE TOILET PAPER HOLDER
2
EVERY HANDICAPPED TOILET TO INCLUDE GAB BARS
3
EACH WASHROOM TO INCLUDE FRAMELESS STEEL
MIRROR (THREE TOTAL)
4
EACH WOMENS TOILET AND TOILET ROOM TO INCLUDE
A SANITARY NAPKIN DISPOSAL (THREE TOTAL)

ROOF PLAN (2)

900 · 600 · 600 · 600 · 600
10000
7600

93.567 EG
93.300   92.625 DG
93.914 EG
93.025 DG
93.425 DG

TYPICAL STEEL GUARD

PAVING SLAB ELEVATION TO BE LEVEL
SLOPES INDICATE SLOPE OF ROOF DECK
BELOW PAVING SLABS TYPICAL

93.650 DG

TYPICAL PAVING SLABS
610X610 MODULES
TOXADA HYDRAPRESSED SLABS BY
ABBOTSFORD CONCRETE OR EQUIVALENT
INSTALL ACCORDING TO MANUFACTURERS
RECOMMENDATIONS AND BEST PRACTICES

93.650 DG
X83.110
X82.470
X82.750
X82.360
X82.210

TYPICAL HANDRAIL

93.650 DG
96.350 DG
TOP OF PAVING SLABS

SLOPE 25% MAX
SLOPE 1.4:1 TYP

PAVING SLAB
LAYOUT TO BE
COORDINATED WITH
DD LOCATIONS TO
PREVENT CONFLICT
WITH PEDESTALS
AND DD TYP

94.630 DG   SLOPE 1.7%   DD 95.300   95.300   SLOPE 1.0%

DOGHOUSE
VENT

LOCATION OF DD

UTILITY
COLUMN

5% SLOPE
MIN TYP

95.350 TS
DN
4R@180
3T@300

94.630 BS   93.375 DG

VENT COVER PLATE OVER
ALL OF DOGHOUSE

SLOPE 25% (MAX)

TYPICAL NOSINGS

93.271 EG
93.375 DG

93.375 DG

TYPICAL HANDRAIL
40MM GALVANIZED STEEL LOCATED
900MM ABOVE FLOOR LEVEL/NOSING
BOTTOM AFFIXED INTO CONCRETE STAIR
TOP AFFIXED TO TYPICAL STEEL GUARD
- SEE DETAIL 8/A7

94.231 EG
93.375 DG

93.380 DG

TYPICAL HANDRAIL
40MM GALVANIZED STEEL LOCATED
900MM ABOVE FLOOR LEVEL/NOSING
BOTTOM AFFIXED INTO CONCRETE STAIR
- SEE DETAIL 1/A7 - SIM
TOP AFFIXED TO TYPICAL DOGHOUSE
WITH 10MM GALVANIZED STEEL TAB

900 · 3230 · 1770 · 5000

ISSUED FOR CONST   MAR 13, 2008
ADDENDUM #2   FEB 28, 2008
ADDENDUM #1   FEB 20, 2008
ISSUED FOR TENDER   JAN 24, 2008
ISSUED FOR DP   JAN 02, 2008
ISSUED FOR DP   DEC 14, 2007
ISSUED FOR COSTING   OCT 16, 2007

Project Title
ROBERT BURNABY
PARK BUILDING

Sheet Title
PLANS

Drawn   lrm
Checked   BC
Job No.   07-14
Date   AUG 2007
Scale   1:50

A3
61

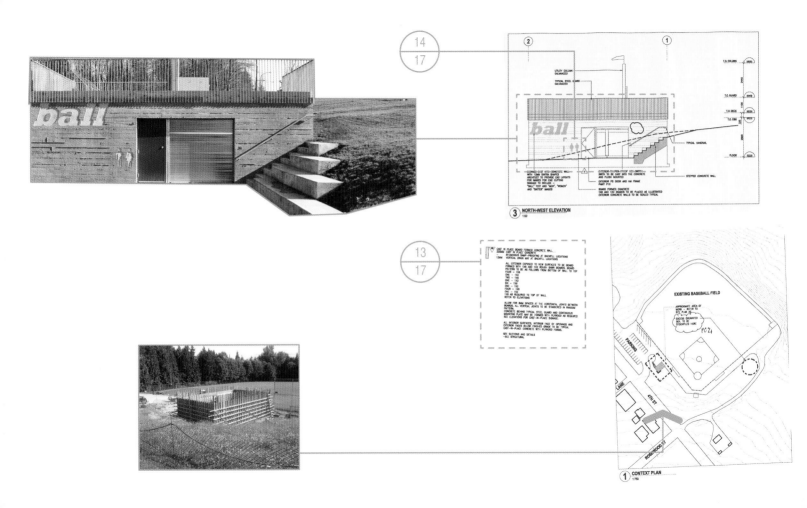

14
17

13
17

NORTH-WEST ELEVATION
3 · 1:50

T.O. COLUMN
T.O. GUARD
T.O. DECK
T.O. CONC.
FLOOR

ball

UTILITY COLUMN
GALVANIZED

TYPICAL STEEL GUARD
GALVANIZED

TYPICAL HANDRAIL

STEPPED CONCRETE WALL

CONTEXT PLAN
1 · 1:750

EXISTING BASEBALL FIELD

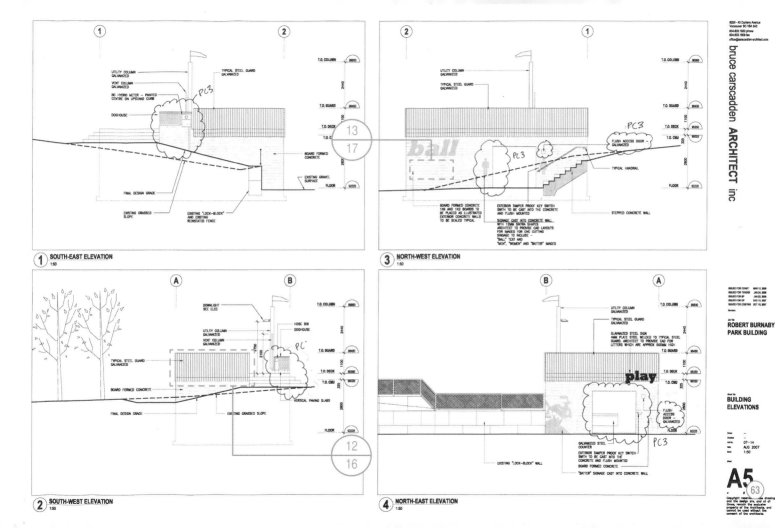

4260 -45 Dunlevy Avenue
Vancouver BC V6A 3A3
604.833.1800 phone
604.833.1809 fax
office@carscadden-architect.com

bruce carscadden ARCHITECT inc

1 SOUTH-EAST ELEVATION 1:50

- UTILITY COLUMN GALVANIZED
- VENT COLUMN GALVANIZED
- BC HYDRO METER — PAINTED CENTRE ON UPSTAND CURB
- DOGHOUSE
- TYPICAL STEEL GUARD GALVANIZED
- PC3
- T.O. COLUMN 98890
- T.O. GUARD 96450
- T.O. DECK 95350
- T.O. C
- BOARD FORMED CONCRETE
- EXISTING GRAVEL SURFACE
- FLOOR 92225
- FINAL DESIGN GRADE
- EXISTING GRASSED SLOPE
- EXISTING "LOCK—BLOCK" AND EXISTING REINSTATED FENCE
- BOARD FORMED CONCRETE 1X8 AND 1X2 BOARDS TO BE PLACED AS ILLUSTRATED EXTERIOR CONCRETE WALLS TO BE SEALED TYPICAL
- 13 / 17

3 NORTH-WEST ELEVATION 1:50

- UTILITY COLUMN GALVANIZED
- TYPICAL STEEL GUARD GALVANIZED
- ball
- PC3
- PC3
- T.O. COLUMN 98890
- T.O. GUARD 96450
- T.O. DECK 95350
- T.O. CMU 95025
- FLOOR 92225
- FLUSH ACCESS DOOR — GALVANIZED
- TYPICAL HANDRAIL
- STEPPED CONCRETE WALL
- EXTERIOR TAMPER PROOF KEY SWITCH SWITH TO BE CAST INTO THE CONCRETE AND FLUSH MOUNTED
- SIGNAGE CAST INTO CONCRETE WALL WITH 12MM SINTRA SHAPES ARCHITECT TO PROVIDE CAD LAYOUTS FOR IMAGES FOR CNC CUTTING SIGNAGE TO INCLUDE "BALL" TEXT AND "MEN", "WOMEN" AND "BATTER" IMAGES

2 SOUTH-WEST ELEVATION 1:50

- DOWNLIGHT SEE ELEC
- UTILITY COLUMN GALVANIZED
- VENT COLUMN GALVANIZED
- HOSE BIB
- DOGHOUSE
- PC
- TYPICAL STEEL GUARD GALVANIZED
- BOARD FORMED CONCRETE
- FINAL DESIGN GRADE
- EXISTING GRASSED SLOPE
- VERTICAL PAVING SLABS
- T.O. COLUMN 98890
- T.O. GUARD 96450
- T.O. DECK 95350
- T.O. CMU 95025
- FLOOR 92225
- 12 / 16

4 NORTH-EAST ELEVATION 1:50

- UTILITY COLUMN GALVANIZED
- TYPICAL STEEL GUARD GALVANIZED
- GALVANIZED STEEL SIGN 4MM PLATE STEEL WELDED TO TYPICAL STEEL GUARD, ARCHITECT TO PROVIDE CAD FOR LETTERS WHICH ARE APPROX 500MM HIGH
- play
- PC3
- T.O. COLUMN 98890
- T.O. GUARD 96450
- T.O. DECK 95350
- T.O. CMU 95025
- FLOOR 92225
- FLUSH ACCESS DOOR — GALVANIZED
- GALVANIZED STEEL COUNTER
- EXTERIOR TAMPER PROOF KEY SWITCH SWITH TO BE CAST INTO THE CONCRETE AND FLUSH MOUNTED
- BOARD FORMED CONCRETE
- "BATTER" SIGNAGE CAST INTO CONCRETE WALL
- EXISTING "LOCK—BLOCK" WALL

ISSUED FOR CONST   MAR 12, 2008
ISSUED FOR TENDER   JAN 24, 2008
ISSUED FOR DP   JAN 22, 2008
ISSUED FOR DP   OCT 16, 2007
ISSUED FOR COSTING   OCT 16, 2007

Revisions

Job Title
ROBERT BURNABY
PARK BUILDING

Sheet Title
BUILDING
ELEVATIONS

Drawn   —
Checked   —
Job No.   07—14
Date   AUG 2007
Scale   1:50

A5

63

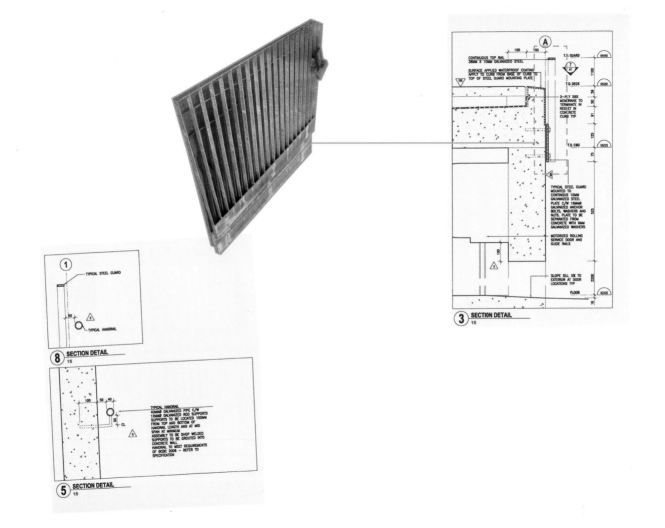

A

CONTINUOUS TOP RAIL
38MM X 10MM GALVANIZED STEEL

SURFACE APPLIED WATERPROOF COATING
APPLY TO CURB FROM BASE OF CURB TO
TOP OF STEEL GUARD MOUNTING PLATE

2-PLY SBS
MEMBRANE TO
TERMINATE IN
REGLET IN
CONCRETE
CURB TYP

TYPICAL STEEL GUARD
MOUNTED TO
CONTINUOUS 10MM
GALVANIZED STEEL
PLATE C/W 18MMØ
GALVANIZED ANCHOR
BOLTS, WASHERS AND
NUTS. PLATE TO BE
SEPARATED FROM
CONCRETE WITH 8MM
GALVANIZED WASHERS

MOTORIZED ROLLING
SERVICE DOOR AND
GUIDE RAILS

SLOPE SILL 5% TO
EXTERIOR AT DOOR
LOCATIONS TYP

FLOOR

3 SECTION DETAIL
1:5

1
TYPICAL STEEL GUARD

TYPICAL HANDRAIL

8 SECTION DETAIL
1:5

TYPICAL HANDRAIL
40MMØ GALVANIZED PIPE C/W
12MMØ GALVANIZED ROD SUPPORTS
SUPPORTS TO BE LOCATED 100MM
FROM TOP AND BOTTOM OF
HANDRAIL LENGTH AND AT MID
SPAN AT MINIMUM
ASSEMBLY TO BE SHOP WELDED
SUPPORTS TO BE GROUTED INTO
CONCRETE WALL
HANDRAIL TO MEET REQUIREMENTS
OF BCBC 2008 - REFER TO
SPECIFICATION

CL

5 SECTION DETAIL
1:5

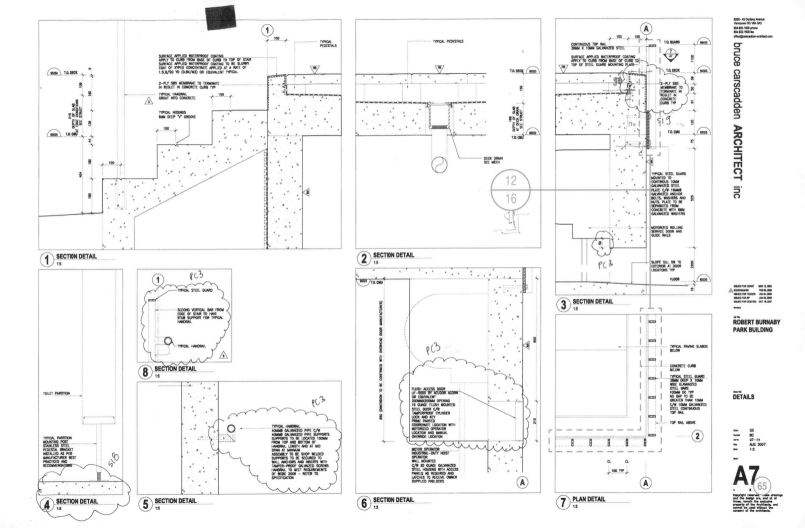

4200 - 45 Dunlevy Avenue
Vancouver BC V6A 3A3
604.633.1630 phone
604.633.1939 fax
office@carscadden-architect.com

bruce carscadden ARCHITECT inc

① SECTION DETAIL 1:5

② SECTION DETAIL 1:5

③ SECTION DETAIL 1:5

④ SECTION DETAIL 1:5

⑤ SECTION DETAIL 1:5

⑥ SECTION DETAIL 1:5

⑦ PLAN DETAIL 1:5

⑧ SECTION DETAIL 1:5

ROBERT BURNABY PARK BUILDING

DETAILS

A7

TERRACE ARENA

CLIENT	The City of Terrace
DESIGN TEAM	Bruce Carscadden Architect, CWMM Consulting Engineers, Bradley Refrigeration, PERC, DIX and Associates, NRS Engineering
PROJECT MANAGER	North American Ice
CONTRACTOR	Genuine Contracting

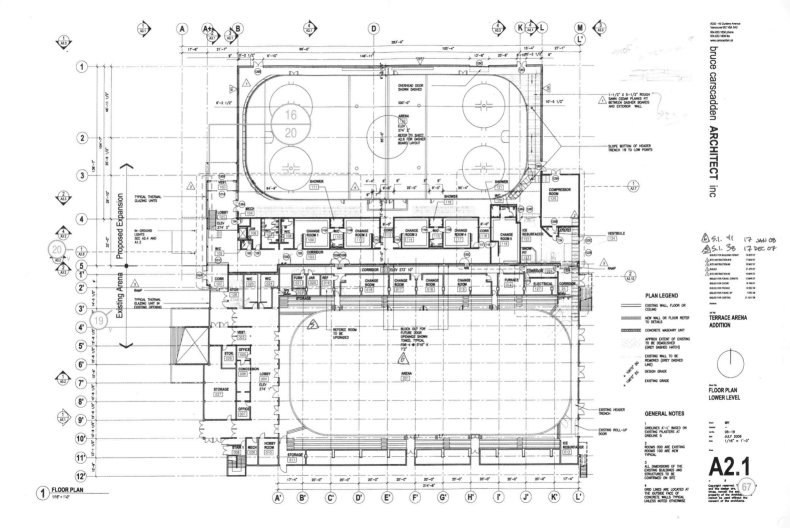

#250 - 40 Dunlevy Avenue
Vancouver BC V6A 3A3
604.633.1830 phone
604.633.1909 fax
www.carscadden.ca

bruce carscadden ARCHITECT inc

ARENA
76J
ELEV
274' 2"
REFER TO SHEET
A2.6 FOR DASHER
BOARD LAYOUT

OVERHEAD DOOR
SHOWN DASHED

1-1/2" X 5-1/2" ROUGH
SAWN CEDAR PLANKS FIT
BETWEEN DASHER BOARDS
AND EXTERIOR WALL

SLOPE BOTTOM OF HEADER
TRENCH 1% TO LOW POINTS

TYPICAL THERMAL
GLAZING UNITS

IN-GROUND
LIGHTS
SEE A2.4 AND
A1.2

TYPICAL THERMAL
GLAZING UNIT IN
EXISTING OPENING

Proposed Expansion

Existing Arena

COMPRESSOR
ROOM
125

VESTIBULE
124

ICE
RESURFACER
122

SNOW
PIT
123

RAMP

PLAN LEGEND

EXISTING WALL, FLOOR OR
CEILING

NEW WALL OR FLOOR REFER
TO DETAILS

CONCRETE MASONRY UNIT

APPROX EXTENT OF EXISTING
TO BE DEMOLISHED
(GREY DASHED HATCH)

EXISTING WALL TO BE
REMOVED (GREY DASHED
LINE)

DESIGN GRADE

EXISTING GRADE

BLOCK OUT FOR
FUTURE DOOR
OPENINGS SHOWN
TONED, TYPICAL
FOR ←→ 3'10"-K
7'2"

REFEREE ROOM
TO BE
UPGRADED

ARENA
001

EXISTING HEADER
TRENCH

EXISTING ROLL-UP
DOOR

ICE
RESURFACER
012

GENERAL NOTES

1
GRIDLINES A'-L' BASED ON
EXISTING PILASTERS AT
GRIDLINE 5

2
ROOMS 000 ARE EXISTING
ROOMS 100 ARE NEW
TYPICAL

3
ALL DIMENSIONS OF THE
EXISTING BUILDINGS AND
STRUCTURES TO BE
CONFIRMED ON SITE

4
GRID LINES ARE LOCATED AT
THE OUTSIDE FACE OF
CONCRETE WALLS TYPICAL
UNLESS NOTED OTHERWISE

S.I. 41   17 JAN 08
S.I. 38   17 DEC 07

ISSUED FOR BUILDING PERMIT   09 NOV 07
SITE INSTRUCTION #41   17 JAN 08
SITE INSTRUCTION #38   18 MAR 07
ISSUED   27 APR 07
SITE INSTRUCTION #40   14 MAY 07
ISSUED FOR FOUND. CONSTR.   12 MAR 07
ISSUED FOR COORD.   05 FEB 07
ISSUED FOR PRICING   14 DEC 06
ISSUED FOR PERMIT   07 DEC 06
ISSUED FOR COSTING   31 JULY 06

Job Title
TERRACE ARENA
ADDITION

Sheet Title
FLOOR PLAN
LOWER LEVEL

Drawn   MH
Checked
Job no.   06-19
Date   JULY 2006
Scale   1/16" = 1'-0"

A2.1

67

FLOOR PLAN
1/16" = 1'-0"

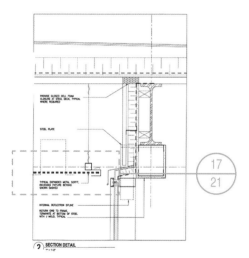

PROVIDE CLOSED CELL FOAM
CLOSURE AT STEEL DECK, TYPICAL,
WHERE REQUIRED

STEEL PLATE

TYPICAL EXPANDED METAL SOFFIT,
RECESSED FIXTURE BEYOND
SHOWN DASHED

INTERNAL DEFLECTION SPLINE

RETURN GWB TO FRAME,
TERMINATE AT BOTTOM OF STEEL
WITH J-MOLD, TYPICAL

17
21

2 SECTION DETAIL
1" = 1'-0"

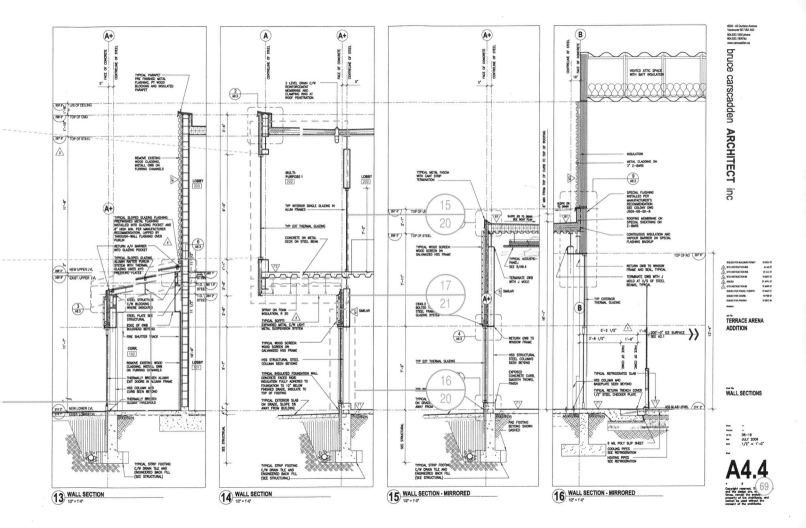

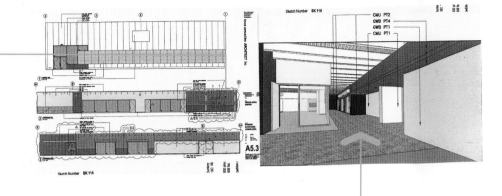

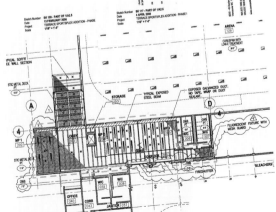

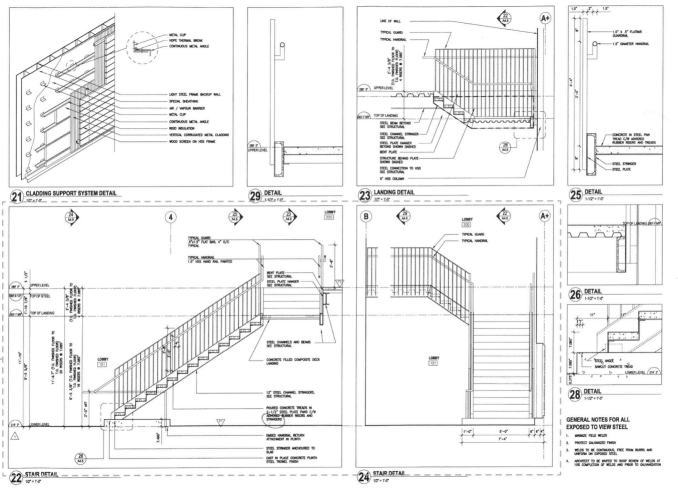

#250 - 45 Dunlevy Avenue
Vancouver BC V6A 3A3
604.633.1800 phone
604.633.1809 fax
www.carscadden.ca

bruce carscadden ARCHITECT inc

21 CLADDING SUPPORT SYSTEM DETAIL
1/2" = 1'-0"

METAL CLIP
HDPE THERMAL BREAK
CONTINUOUS METAL ANGLE

LIGHT STEEL FRAME BACKUP WALL
SPECIAL SHEATHING
AIR / VAPOUR BARRIER
METAL CLIP
CONTINUOUS METAL ANGLE
RIGID INSULATION
VERTICAL CORRUGATED METAL CLADDING
WOOD SCREEN ON HSS FRAME

29 DETAIL
1-1/2" = 1'-0"

UPPER LEVEL

UPPER LEVEL

23 LANDING DETAIL
1/2" = 1'-2"

LINE OF WALL
TYPICAL GUARD
TYPICAL GUARD

UPPER LEVEL

TOP OF LANDING
STEEL BEAM BEYOND
SEE STRUCTURAL
STEEL CHANNEL STRINGER
SEE STRUCTURAL
STEEL PLATE HANGER
BEYOND SHOWN DASHED
BENT PLATE
STRUCTURE BEHIND PLATE
SHOWN DASHED
STEEL CONNECTION TO HSS
SEE STRUCTURAL
6" HSS COLUMN

25 DETAIL
1-1/2" = 1'-0"

1.5" X .5" FLATBAR
GUARDRAIL
1.5" DIAMETER HANDRAIL

CONCRETE IN STEEL PAN
TREAD C/W ADHERED
RUBBER RISERS AND TREADS

STEEL STRINGER
STEEL PLATE

22 STAIR DETAIL
1/2" = 1'-0"

LOBBY 200

TYPICAL GUARD
.5"x1.5" FLAT BAR 4" O/C
TYPICAL

TYPICAL HANDRAIL
1.5" HSS HAND RAIL PAINTED

UPPER LEVEL
TOP OF STEEL
TOP OF LANDING

BENT PLATE
STEEL PLATE HANGER
SEE STRUCTURAL

LOBBY 101

STEEL CHANNELS AND BEAMS
SEE STRUCTURAL

CONCRETE FILLED COMPOSITE DECK
LANDING

12" STEEL CHANNEL STRINGERS,
SEE STRUCTURAL

POURED CONCRETE TREADS IN
2-1/2" STEEL PLATE PANS C/W
ADHERED RUBBER RISERS AND
STRINGERS

LOWER LEVEL

EMBED HANDRAIL RETURN
ATTACHMENT IN PLINTH
STEEL STRINGER ANCHORED TO
SLAB
CAST IN PLACE CONCRETE PLINTH
STEEL TROWEL FINISH

24 STAIR DETAIL
1/2" = 1'-0"

LOBBY 200

TYPICAL GUARD
TYPICAL HANDRAIL

LOBBY 101

LOWER LEVEL

26 DETAIL
1-1/2" = 1'-0"

TOP OF LANDING

28 DETAIL
1-1/2" = 1'-0"

STEEL ANGLE
SAWCUT CONCRETE TREAD

LOWER LEVEL

ISSUED FOR BUILDING PERMIT   16 NOV 07
SITE INSTRUCTION #6   15 MAY 07
ISSUED   27 APR 07
Revisions

TERRACE ARENA
ADDITION

WALL SECTIONS

Drawn   --
Checked   --
Job No.   06-19
Date   JULY 2006
Scale   AS NOTED

A4.6

71

GENERAL NOTES FOR ALL
EXPOSED TO VIEW STEEL

1. MINIMIZE FIELD WELDS

2. PROTECT GALVANIZED FINISH

3. WELDS TO BE CONTINUOUS, FREE FROM BURRS AND
   UNIFORM ON EXPOSED STEEL

4. ARCHITECT TO BE INVITED TO SHOP REVIEW OF WELDS AT
   10% COMPLETION OF WELDS AND PRIOR TO GALVANIZATION

WINFIELD ARENA DRESSING ROOMS

CLIENT — The District of Lake Country
DESIGN TEAM — Bruce Carscadden Architect, CWMM Consulting Engineers, Jade West Engineering, The MMM Group, PERC, Tracy Penner Landscape Architect
CONTRACTOR — CorWest Builders

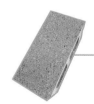

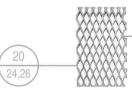

20
24,26

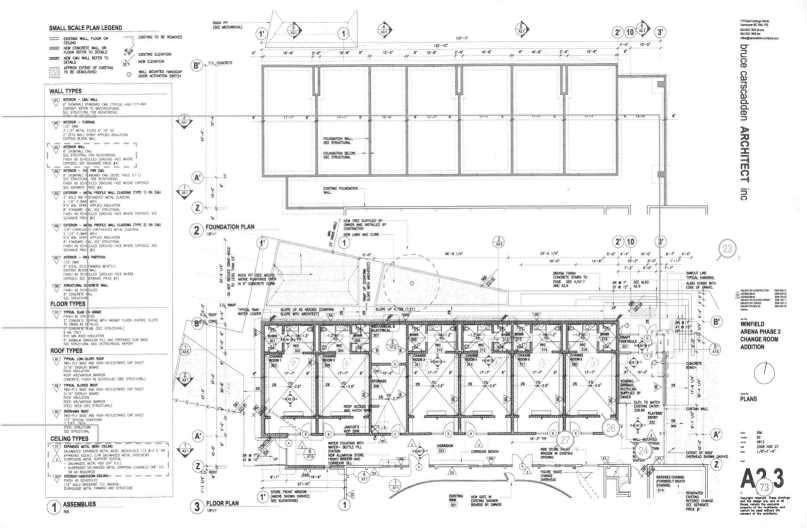

SMALL SCALE PLAN LEGEND

- ▭▭▭ EXISTING WALL, FLOOR OR CEILING
- ▨▨▨ NEW CONCRETE WALL OR FLOOR REFER TO DETAILS
- ▧▧▧ NEW CMU WALL REFER TO DETAILS
- ▨▨▨ APPROX EXTENT OF EXISTING TO BE DEMOLISHED
- ▭▭▭ EXISTING TO BE REMOVED
- ⊿ EXISTING ELEVATION
- ⊿ NEW ELEVATION
- ⬤ WALL MOUNTED HANDICAP DOOR ACTIVATION SWITCH

WALL TYPES

W1 INTERIOR – CMU WALL
8" (NOMINAL) STANDARD CMU (TYPICAL HIGH FLY-ASH CONTENT; REFER TO SPECIFICATIONS)
SEE STRUCTURAL FOR REINFORCING
FINISH AS SCHEDULED

W2 INTERIOR – FURRING
1/2" GWB
3 1/2" METAL STUDS AT 16" OC
2" (R10 MIN) SPRAY APPLIED INSULATION
EXISTING BLOCK WALL

W3 INTERIOR WALL
8" (NOMINAL) CMU
SEE STRUCTURAL FOR REINFORCING
FINISH AS SCHEDULED (GROUND FACE WHERE EXPOSED, SEE SEPARATE PRICE #4)

W4 INTERIOR – 1 HR FRR CMU
8" (NOMINAL) STANDARD CMU (BCBC TABLE 2.1.1)
SEE STRUCTURAL FOR REINFORCING
FINISH AS SCHEDULED (GROUND FACE WHERE EXPOSED, SEE SEPARATE PRICE #4)

W5 EXTERIOR – METAL PROFILE WALL CLADDING (TYPE 1) ON CMU
3" BOLD RIB PREFINISHED METAL CLADDING
2 1/2" Z-BARS WITH
R10 MIN. SPRAY APPLIED INSULATION
8" STANDARD CMU, SEE STRUCTURAL
FINISH AS SCHEDULED (GROUND FACE WHERE EXPOSED, SEE SEPARATE PRICE #4)

W6 EXTERIOR – METAL PROFILE WALL CLADDING (TYPE 2) ON CMU
7/8" CORRUGATED PREFINISHED METAL CLADDING
2 1/2" Z-BARS WITH
R10 MIN. SPRAY APPLIED INSULATION
8" STANDARD CMU, SEE STRUCTURAL
FINISH AS SCHEDULED (GROUND FACE WHERE EXPOSED, SEE SEPARATE PRICE #4)

W7 INTERIOR – GWU PARTITION
1/2" GWB
6" STEEL STUD FRAMING @16"O.C.
EXISTING BLOCK WALL
FINISH AS SCHEDULED (GROUND FACE WHERE EXPOSED, SEE SEPARATE PRICE #4)

W8 STRUCTURAL CONCRETE WALL
FINISH AS SCHEDULED
8" CONCRETE WALL
SEE STRUCTURAL

FLOOR TYPES

F1 TYPICAL SLAB ON GRADE
FINISH AS SPECIFIED
2" CONCRETE TOPPING WITH RADIANT FLOOR HEATING; SLOPE TO DRAIN AS DETAILED
"CONCRETE" SLAB, (SEE STRUCTURAL)
6 MIL POLY
R10 MIN RIGID INSULATION
6" MINIMUM GRANULAR FILL AND PREPARED SUB-BASE
SEE STRUCTURAL AND GEOTECHNICAL REPORT

ROOF TYPES

R1 TYPICAL LOW-SLOPE ROOF
TWO-PLY BASE AND HIGH-REFLECTANCE CAP SHEET
3/16" OVERLAY BOARD
RIGID INSULATION
ROOF AIR/VAPOUR BARRIER
CONCRETE, FINISH AS SCHEDULED (SEE STRUCTURAL)

R2 TYPICAL SLOPED ROOF
TWO-PLY BASE AND HIGH-REFLECTANCE CAP SHEET
3/16" OVERLAY BOARD
RIGID INSULATION
ROOF AIR/VAPOUR BARRIER
STEEL DECK (SEE STRUCTURAL)

R3 OVERHANG ROOF
TWO-PLY BASE AND HIGH-REFLECTANCE CAP SHEET
1/2" SPECIAL SHEATHING
3 STEEL DECK
STEEL STRUCTURE
SEE STRUCTURAL

CEILING TYPES

C1 EXPANDED METAL MESH CEILING
GALVANIZED EXPANDED METAL (MONICHOLS 1/2 #13 S, OR APPROVED EQUIV.) C/W GALVANIZED METAL FASTENERS
SUSPENDED METAL SUPPORT SYSTEM
- GALVANIZED METAL HSS (24" O.C.)
- SUSPENDED GALVANIZED METAL CARRYING CHANNELS (48" O.C. OR AS REQUIRED)

C2 INTERIOR WASHROOM CEILING
FINISH AS SCHEDULED
1/2" MOLD RESISTANT TILE BACKER
SUSPENDED METAL FRAMING AND STRUCTURE

(1) ASSEMBLIES
N/A

(2) FOUNDATION PLAN
1/8"=1'

(3) FLOOR PLAN
1/8"=1'

715 East Hastings Street
Vancouver BC V6A 1R8
604.633.1800 phone
604.633.1809 fax
office@carscadden-architect.com

bruce carscadden ARCHITECT inc

WINFIELD
ARENA PHASE 2
CHANGE ROOM
ADDITION

Job No. 0812
Date 2008 NOV 27
Scale 1/8"=1'-0"

PLANS

A2.3

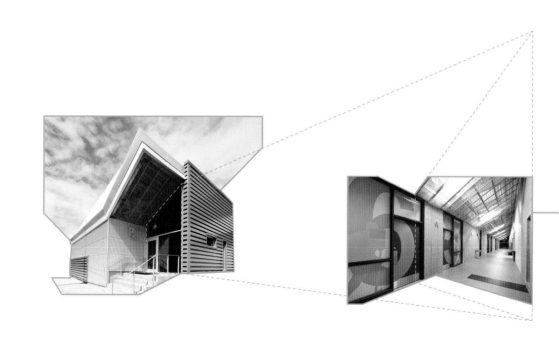

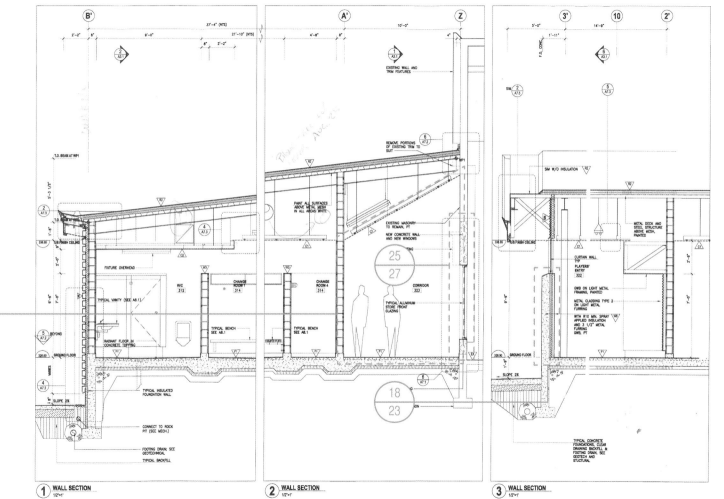

715 East Hastings Street
Vancouver BC V6A 1R3
604.633.1830 phone
604.633.1839 fax
office@carscadden-architect.com

bruce carscadden ARCHITECT inc

ISSUED FOR CONSTRUCTION 2009 MAR 31
ISSUED FOR BUILDING PERMIT 2009 FEB 11
ISSUED FOR TENDER 2008 FEB 10
ISSUED FOR 90% DB 2008 NOV 28
Revisions

**WINFIELD
ARENA PHASE 2
CHANGE ROOM
ADDITION**

WALL SECTIONS

Drawn   RM
Checked   BC
Job No.   0812
Date   2008 NOV 27
Scale   1/2"=1'-0"

A5.1

---

1 WALL SECTION 1/2"=1'

2 WALL SECTION 1/2"=1'

3 WALL SECTION 1/2"=1'

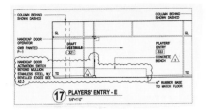

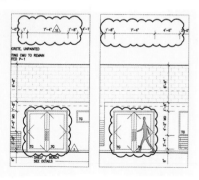

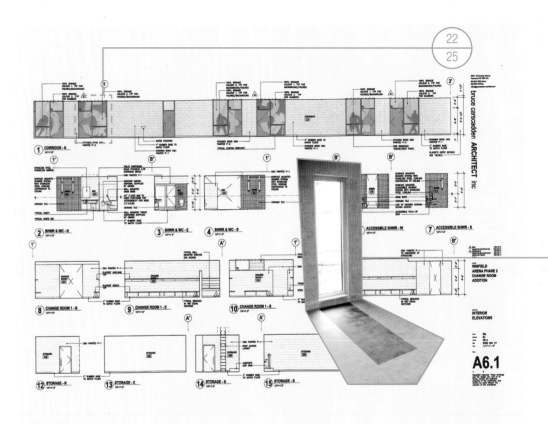

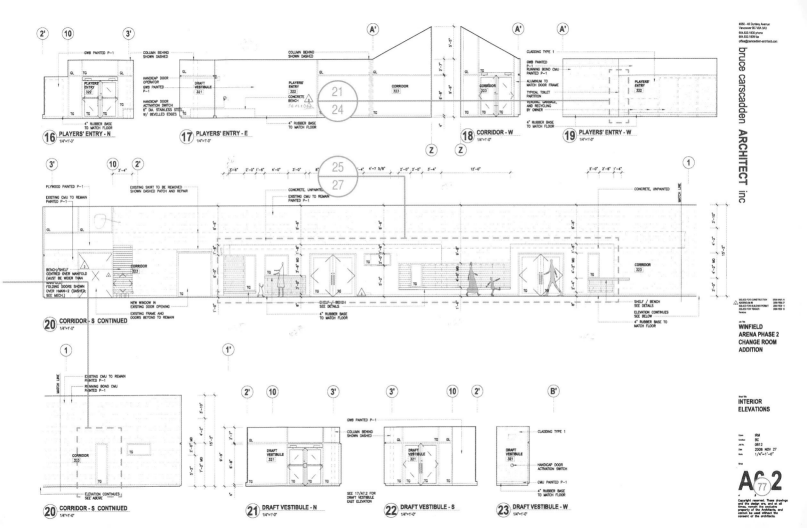

#260 - 46 Dunlevy Avenue
Vancouver BC V6A 3A3
604.633.1800 phone
604.633.1809 fax
office@carscadden-architect.com

bruce carscadden ARCHITECT inc

16 PLAYERS' ENTRY - N
1/4"=1'-0"

17 PLAYERS' ENTRY - E
1/4"=1'-0"

18 CORRIDOR - W
1/4"=1'-0"

19 PLAYERS' ENTRY - W
1/4"=1'-0"

20 CORRIDOR - S CONTINUED
1/4"=1'-0"

20 CORRIDOR - S CONTINUED
1/4"=1'-0"

21 DRAFT VESTIBULE - N
1/4"=1'-0"

22 DRAFT VESTIBULE - S
1/4"=1'-0"

23 DRAFT VESTIBULE - W
1/4"=1'-0"

WINFIELD
ARENA PHASE 2
CHANGE ROOM
ADDITION

INTERIOR
ELEVATIONS

Drawn   IRM
Checked   BC
Job No.   0612
Date   2008 NOV 27
Scale   1/4"=1'-0"

A6.2
of 77

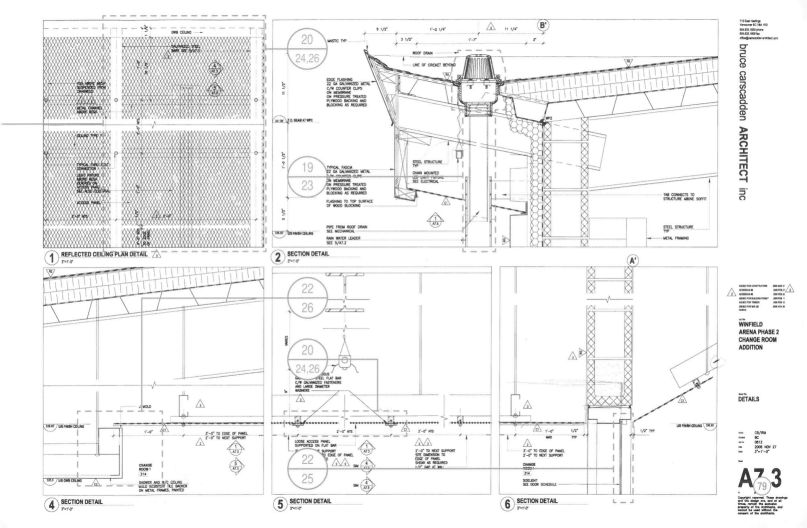

710 East Hastings
Vancouver BC V6A 1R3
604.633.1830 phone
604.633.1809 fax
office@carscadden-architect.com

bruce carscadden ARCHITECT inc

1 REFLECTED CEILING PLAN DETAIL
3"=1'-0"

GWB CEILING

GALVANIZED STEEL
BARS SEE 5/A7.3

FGS ABOVE MESH
SUSPENDED FROM
CHANNELS

METAL CHANNEL
ABOVE MESH

TYPICAL (THRU-BOLT)
CONNECTION TO
MAIN FIXING
ABOVE MESH
SEE ALSO ELECTRICAL

ACCESS PANEL

2 SECTION DETAIL
3"=1'-0"

20
24,26

MASTIC TYP

ROOF DRAIN

LINE OF CRICKET BEYOND

EDGE FLASHING
22 GA GALVANIZED METAL
C/W COUNTER CLIPS
ON MEMBRANE
ON PRESSURE TREATED
PLYWOOD BACKING AND
BLOCKING AS REQUIRED

T.O. BEAM AT WP2

STEEL STRUCTURE
TYP

CHAIN MOUNTED
LED LIGHT FIXTURE
SEE ELECTRICAL

19
23

TYPICAL FASCIA
22 GA GALVANIZED METAL
C/W COUNTER CLIPS
ON MEMBRANE
ON PRESSURE TREATED
PLYWOOD BACKING AND
BLOCKING AS REQUIRED

FLASHING TO TOP SURFACE
OF WOOD BLOCKING

U/S FINISH CEILING

PIPE FROM ROOF DRAIN
SEE MECHANICAL

RAIN WATER LEADER
SEE 5/A7.2

TAB CONNECTS TO
STRUCTURE ABOVE SOFFIT

STEEL STRUCTURE
TYP

METAL FRAMING

4 SECTION DETAIL
3"=1'-0"

J MOLD

U/S FINISH CEILING

U/S GWB CEILING

CHANGE
ROOM 1
314

1'-0"

3'-0" TO EDGE OF PANEL
2'-0" TO NEXT SUPPORT

SHOWER AND W/C CEILING
MOLD 'RESISTANT' TILE BACKER
ON METAL FRAMES, PAINTED

5 SECTION DETAIL
3"=1'-0"

22
26

20
24,26

CONTINUOUS
GALVANIZED STEEL FLAT BAR
C/W GALVANIZED FASTENERS
AND LARGE DIAMETER
WASHERS

LOOSE ACCESS PANEL
SUPPORTED ON FLAT BAR

2'-0" TO EDGE OF PANEL

22
25

2'-0" NTS

2'-0" NTS

3'-0" TO NEXT SUPPORT
SITE DIMENSION TO
EDGE OF PANEL
SHEAR AS REQUIRED
1/2" GAP AT WALL

SIM

SIM

6 SECTION DETAIL
3"=1'-0"

3'-0" TO EDGE OF PANEL
2'-0" TO NEXT SUPPORT

CHANGE
ROOM 1
314

SIDELIGHT
SEE DOOR SCHEDULE

U/S FINISH CEILING

1'-0"   1/2"
MAX   TYP

1/2" TYP

ISSUED FOR CONSTRUCTION   2009 MAR 31
ADDENDUM #2   2009 FEB 27
ADDENDUM #1   2009 FEB 23
ISSUED FOR BUILDING PERMIT   2009 FEB 11
ISSUED FOR TENDER   2009 FEB 13
ISSUED FOR 50% DD   2008 NOV 26

Job Title
WINFIELD
ARENA PHASE 2
CHANGE ROOM
ADDITION

Sheet Title
DETAILS

Drawn   CB/IRM
Checked   BC
Job No.   0812
Date   2008 NOV 27
Scale   3"=1'-0"

A7.3
79

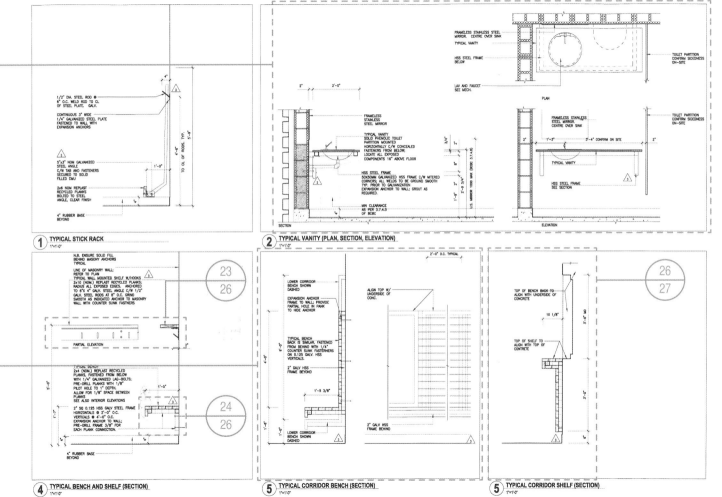

1 TYPICAL STICK RACK
1"=1'-0"

2 TYPICAL VANITY (PLAN, SECTION, ELEVATION)
1"=1'-0"

4 TYPICAL BENCH AND SHELF (SECTION)
1"=1'-0"

5 TYPICAL CORRIDOR BENCH (SECTION)
1"=1'-0"

5 TYPICAL CORRIDOR SHELF (SECTION)
1"=1'-0"

bruce carscadden ARCHITECT inc

#250 – 45 Dunlevy Avenue
Vancouver BC V6A 3A3
604.633.1800 phone
604.633.1809 fax
office@carscadden-architect.com

ISSUED FOR CONSTRUCTION   2008 MAR 31
ADDENDUM #2   2009 FEB 27
ISSUED FOR BUILDING PERMIT   2009 FEB 11
ISSUED FOR TENDER   2009 FEB 10

WINFIELD
ARENA PHASE 2
CHANGE ROOM
ADDITION

Sheet Title
MILLWORK

Drawn   IRM
Checked   BC
Job No   0812
Date   2008 NOV 27
Scale   1"=1'-0"

Sheet

A8.1
81

RENFREW COMMUNITY CENTRE RENOVATIONS

CLIENT The City of Vancouver
DESIGN TEAM Bruce Carscadden Architect, CY Loh & Associates, The AME Consulting Group, The MMM Group
CONTRACTOR Parkwood Construction

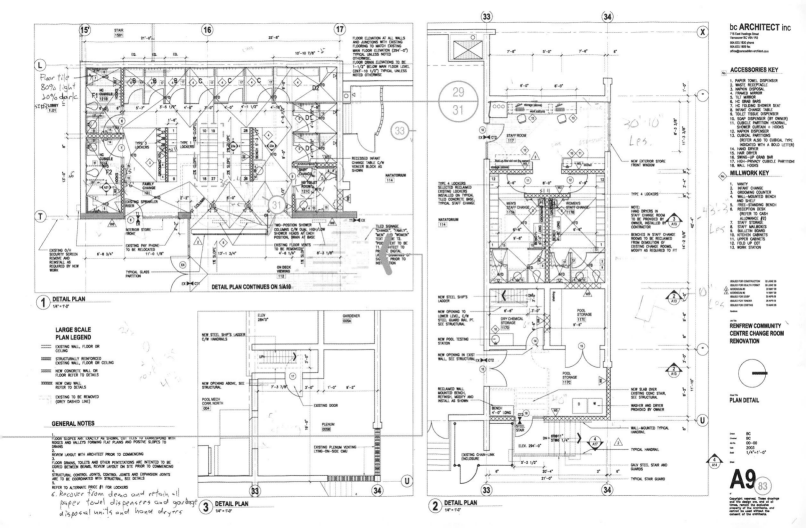

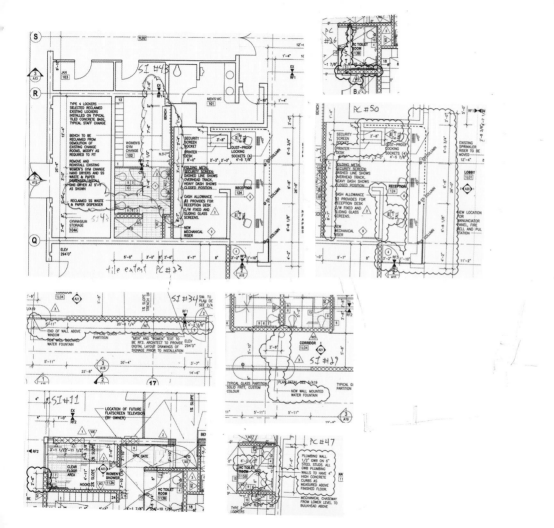

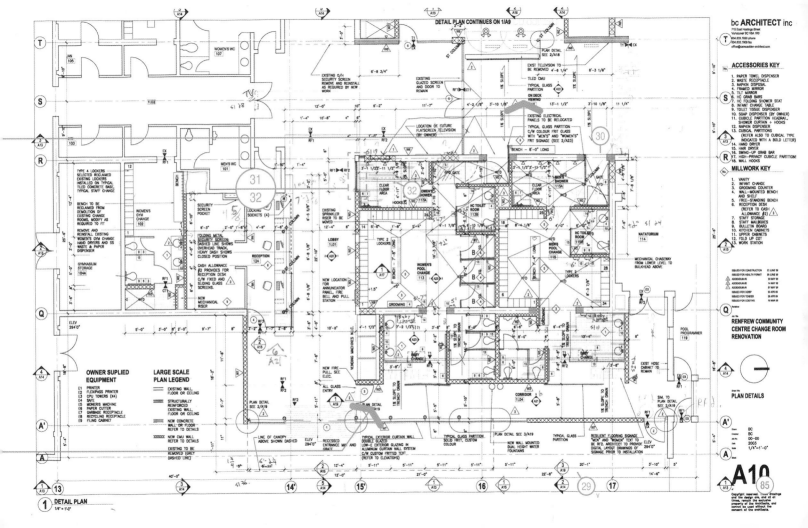

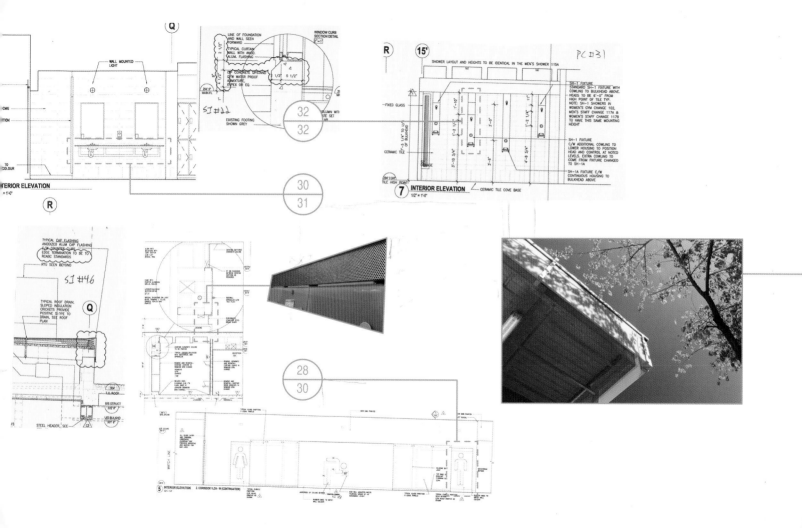

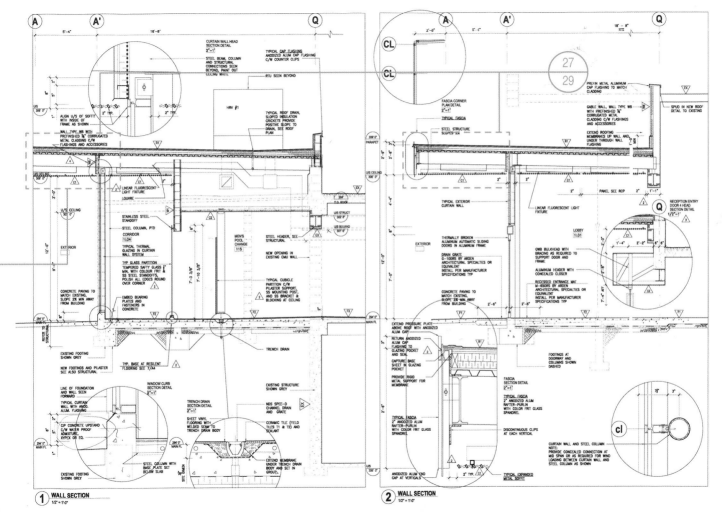

PENTICTON AQUATIC CENTRE

CLIENT	The City of Penticton
DESIGN TEAM	Bruce Carscadden Architect, Mieklejohn Architects, Read Jones Christofferson, The AME Consulting Group, Applied Engineering Solutions, The Iredale Group, PERC, Recollective Consulting
PROJECT MANAGERS	Pivotal Project Management, Speigel Skillen and Associates
CONSTRUCTION MANAGER	Stuart Olson Dominion Construction

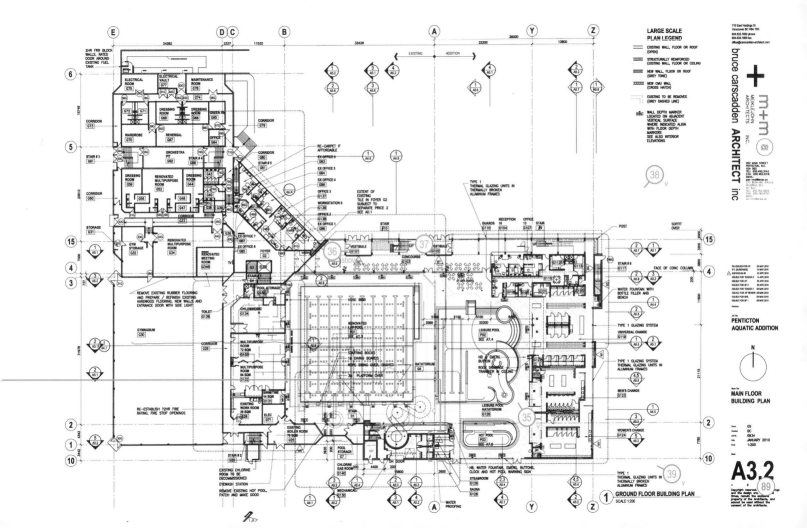

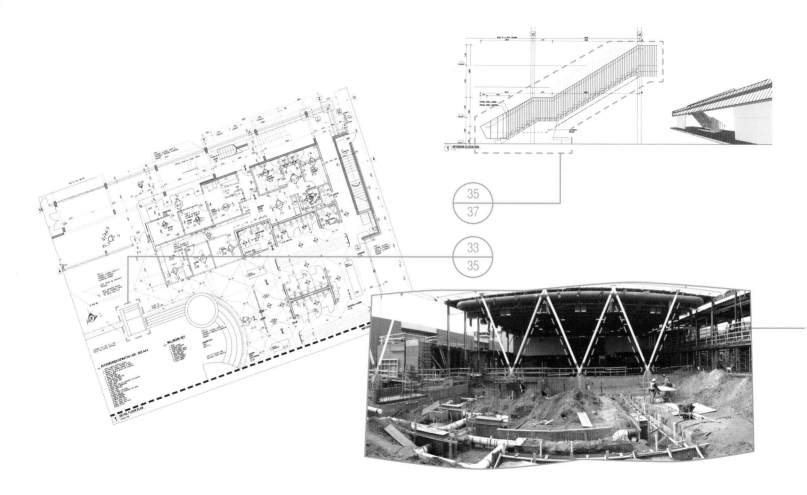

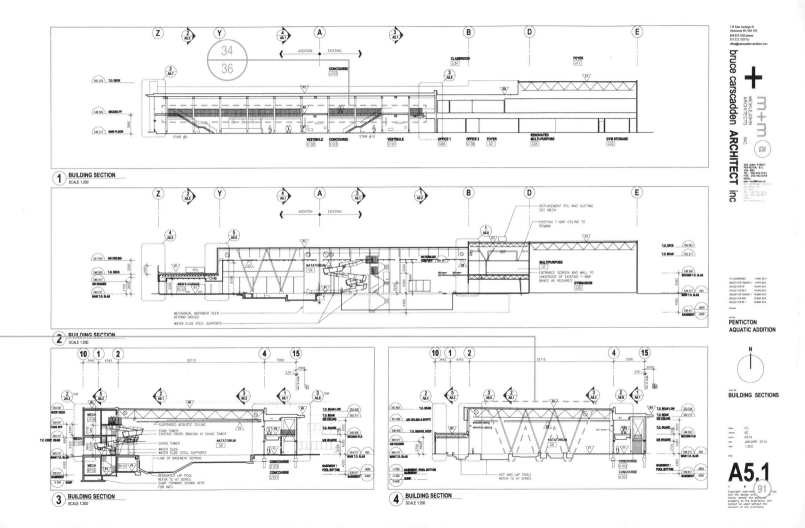

715 East Hastings St
Vancouver BC V6A 1R3
604 633 1830 phone
604 633 1826 fax
office@carscadden-architect.com

bruce carscadden ARCHITECT inc

MEIKLEJOHN ARCHITECTS INC.

262 MAIN STREET
PENTICTON, B.C.
V2A 5B2
TEL: 250.492.3143
FAX: 250.492.0316

PENTICTON
AQUATIC ADDITION

BUILDING SECTIONS

A5.1

91

1 BUILDING SECTION
   SCALE 1:200

2 BUILDING SECTION
   SCALE 1:200

3 BUILDING SECTION
   SCALE 1:200

4 BUILDING SECTION
   SCALE 1:200

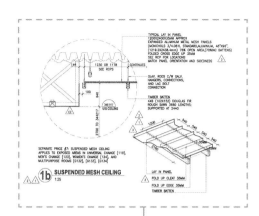

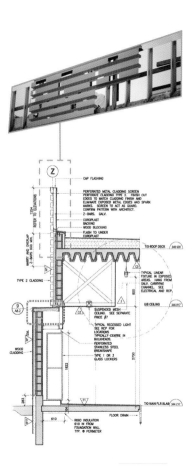

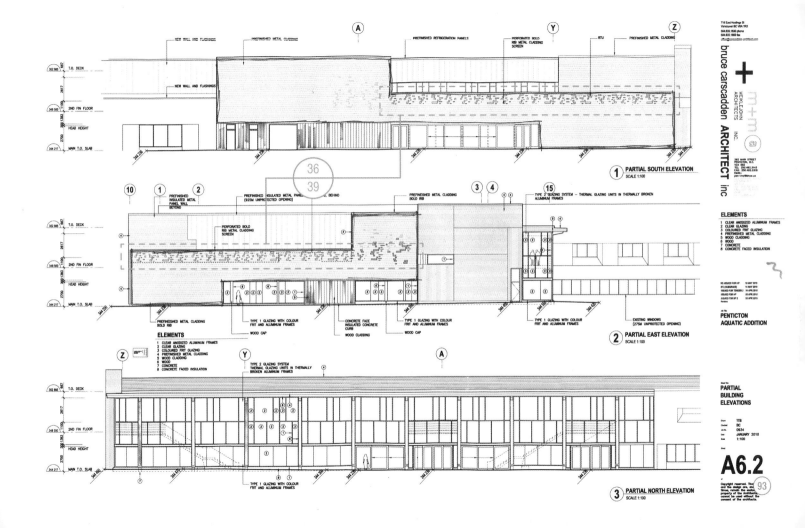

715 East Hastings St
Vancouver BC V6A 1R3
604.633.1630 phone
604.633.1659 fax
office@meiklejohn-architect.com

bruce carscadden ARCHITECT inc

m+m
MEIKLEJOHN
ARCHITECTS
INC.

262 MAIN STREET
PENTICTON, B.C.
V2A 5B2
TEL: 250.492.3443
FAX: 250.492.0319
EMAIL:
pen-m@telus.net

PARTIAL SOUTH ELEVATION
SCALE 1:100 — 1

PARTIAL EAST ELEVATION
SCALE 1:100 — 2

PARTIAL NORTH ELEVATION
SCALE 1:100 — 3

ELEMENTS
1 CLEAR ANODIZED ALUMINUM FRAMES
2 CLEAR GLAZING
3 COLOURED FRIT GLAZING
4 PREFINISHED METAL CLADDING
5 WOOD CLADDING
6 WOOD
7 CONCRETE
8 CONCRETE FACED INSULATION

ELEMENTS
1 CLEAR ANODIZED ALUMINUM FRAMES
2 CLEAR GLAZING
3 COLOURED FRIT GLAZING
4 PREFINISHED METAL CLADDING
5 WOOD CLADDING
6 WOOD
7 CONCRETE
8 CONCRETE FACED INSULATION

ELEMENTS
1 CLEAR ANODIZED ALUMINUM FRAMES
2 CLEAR GLAZING
3 COLOURED FRIT GLAZING
4 PREFINISHED METAL CLADDING
5 WOOD CLADDING
6 WOOD
7 CONCRETE
8 CONCRETE FACED INSULATION

**PENTICTON
AQUATIC ADDITION**

**PARTIAL
BUILDING
ELEVATIONS**

Drawn TTB
Checked BC
Job No. 0934
Date JANUARY 2010
Scale 1:100

A6.2

93

CHANGE CUBICLE SCHEDULE

DRY CHANGE CUBICLE

B
SMALL FAMILY CHANGE

WALL MOUNTED BENCH WITH HOOKS AND BAR SHELF OVER

HIGH PRIVACY PARTITION WHERE SPECIFIED IN DRAWINGS

C
LARGE FAMILY CHANGE

5'0" WHEELCHAIR TURNING RADIUS, EXTENDS UNDER WALL MOUNTED BENCH, SHOWN DASHED BENCH HAS HOOKS AND BAR SHELF OVER

HIGH PRIVACY PARTITION

WET CHANGE CUBICLE

D1
LARGE FAMILY CHANGE

ALL CMU WALLS IN SHOWER AREA (SHOWN DASHED) TO RECEIVE FLOOR-TO-CEILING T3 TILE

WALL MOUNTED BENCH WITH HOOKS AND BAR SHELF OVER

HIGH PRIVACY PARTITION

D2
LARGE FAMILY CHANGE

ALL CMU WALLS IN SHOWER AREA (SHOWN DASHED) TO RECEIVE FLOOR-TO-CEILING T3 TILE

WALL MOUNTED BENCH WITH HOOKS AND BAR SHELF OVER

HIGH PRIVACY PARTITION

CEILING OR BULKHEAD OVER BENCH SHOWN DASHED, SEE DRAWINGS

UNIVERSAL WET CHANGE ROOM
MIN. CLEARANCES AS PER VBBL DIV. 3.8

F1
UNIVERSAL CHANGE ROOM

HC SHOWER STALL C/W HC FOLDING SHOWER SEAT, HC GRAB BARS, AND HC WALL SHOWER

SWING UP GRAB BAR

HOOKS AND BAR SHELF

HM DOOR AND SIDELIGHT C/W FROSTED GLAZING

WALL MOUNTED VANITY AND MIRROR, NO SUPPORT UNDER SEE DETAILS

ALL CMU WALLS IN CUBICLE TO RECEIVE FLOOR-TO-CEILING T3 TILE

F2
UNIVERSAL CHANGE ROOM

WALL MOUNTED VANITY AND MIRROR, NO SUPPORT UNDER SEE DETAILS

HM DOOR AND SIDELIGHT C/W FROSTED GLAZING

HOOKS AND BAR SHELF

SWING UP GRAB BARS

HC SHOWER STALL

ALL CMU WALLS IN CUBICLE TO RECEIVE FLOOR-TO-CEILING T3 TILE

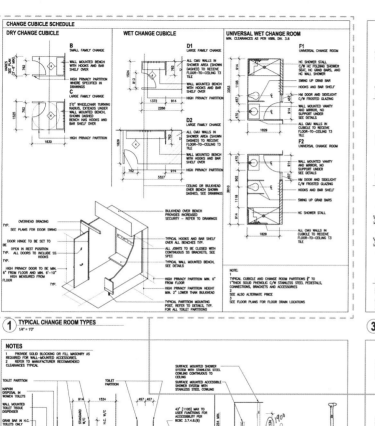

OVERHEAD BRACING

TYP. SEE PLANS FOR DOOR SWING

DOOR HINGE TO BE SET TO BE OPEN IN REST POSITION

TYP. ALL DOORS TO USE SS HOOKS

HIGH PRIVACY DOOR TO BE MIN. 6" FROM FLOOR AND MIN. 6'-10" HIGH MEASURED FROM FLOOR

BULKHEAD OVER BENCH PROVIDES INCREASED SECURITY — REFER TO DRAWINGS

TYPICAL HOOKS AND BAR SHELF OVER ALL BENCHES TYP.

ALL JOINTS TO BE CLOSED WITH CONTINUOUS SS BRACKETS, SEE SPEC

TYPICAL WALL MOUNTED BENCH, SEE DETAILS

HIGH PRIVACY PARTITION MIN. 6" FROM FLOOR

HIGH PRIVACY PARTITION HEIGHT MIN. 2" LOWER THAN BULKHEAD

TYPICAL PARTITION MOUNTING POST, REFER TO DETAILS, TYP. FOR ALL TOILET PARTITIONS

NOTE:
1 TYPICAL CUBICLE AND CHANGE ROOM PARTITIONS ¾" TO 1" THICK SOLID PHENOLIC C/W STAINLESS STEEL PEDESTALS, CONNECTIONS, BRACKETS AND ACCESSORIES
2 SEE ALSO ALTERNATE PRICE
3 SEE FLOOR PLANS FOR FLOOR DRAIN LOCATIONS

1 TYPICAL CHANGE ROOM TYPES
1/4" = 1'0"

NOTES

1 PROVIDE SOLID BLOCKING OR FILL MASONRY AS REQUIRED FOR WALL-MOUNTED ACCESSORIES.
2 REFER TO MANUFACTURER RECOMMENDED CLEARANCES TYPICAL

TOILET PARTITION

NAPKIN DISPOSAL IN WOMEN TOILETS

WALL MOUNTED TOILET TISSUE DISPENSER

GRAB BAR IN H.C. TOILETS ONLY

TOILET PARTITION

STANDARD W/C

H.C. W/C

SURFACE MOUNTED SHOWER SYSTEM WITH STAINLESS STEEL COMLING CONTINUOUS TO CEILING

SURFACE MOUNTED ACCESSIBLE SHOWER SYSTEM WITH STAINLESS STEEL COMLING

43" [1100] MAX TO USER FUNCTIONS FOR ACCESSIBILITY PER BCBC 3.7.4.8.(8)

TILE ON CMU AT ALL URINAL LOCATIONS. SEE SPECIFICATION

CLEARANCE FOR WHEELCHAIR KEEP PLUMBING CLEAR

2 TYPICAL WASHROOM MOUNTING HEIGHTS
1/4" = 1'0"

TYPICAL SOLID PHENOLIC LOCKER TOP AND GABLE SEE PLAN AND SECTIONS

DOUBLE TIER, FREE-STANDING ISLAND LOCKERS, DOUBLE BANK

CONCRETE CURB WITH COVE BASE AS SCHEDULED

ELEVATION   SECTION

LOCKER TYPE 1

STAINLESS STEEL DOOR AND BODY DOUBLE TIER OR SINGLE TIER AS SHOWN C/W LOCKING MECHANISM AS SPECIFIED

CONCRETE CURB WITH COVE BASE AS SCHEDULED

ELEVATION   SECTION

LOCKER TYPE 2

TYPICAL SOLID PHENOLIC LOCKER TOP, BOTTOM, AND GABLE WHERE REQUIRED

TYPICAL ACCESSIBLE LOCKERS C/W

KEY HOLDER: EASY-TO-GRIP, HEAVY-DUTY CURVED HANDLE PROVIDING EXTRA LEVERAGE FOR TURNING KEY.

DOOR GRIP: LOOP DESIGN PROJECTING FROM LOCKER FACE OPERABLE WITH ONE HAND WITHOUT TWISTING WRIST.

DECAL: INTERNATIONAL ACCESSIBILITY DECAL AFFIXED TO DOOR

2'-6" MIN CLEAR FLOOR SPACE

4'-0" MIN CLEAR FLOOR SPACE

ELEVATION   SECTION

LOCKER TYPE 3

LOCKER TYPE 4 IS RECLAIMED FROM DEMOLITION OF EXISTING CHANGE FACILITIES. REPAIR AS REQUIRED.

NOTE:
TYPICAL LOCKERS STAINLESS STEEL CONSTRUCTION C/W HASP LOCKING MECHANISMS SEE ALSO ALTERNATE PRICE

3 TYPICAL LOCKER TYPES
1/4" = 1'0"

GENERAL NOTES

1. THE USE OF THESE DRAWINGS IS LIMITED TO THE COLUMN MARKED ISSUED IN THE TITLE BLOCK OF EACH SHEET. DO NOT CONSTRUCT FROM THESE DRAWINGS UNLESS MARKED ISSUED FOR CONSTRUCTION

2. THESE DRAWINGS TO BE READ IN CONJUNCTION WITH THE PROJECT MANUAL AND SPECIFICATIONS

3. PROVIDE FIRE STOPS TO VBBL REQUIREMENTS 3.1.9 AND 3.1.11

4. WATERPROOF MEMBRANE TO BE APPLIED TO SHOWER FLOORS.

5. ALL TILE TYP. THINSET (U.N.O.)

6. PROVIDE TILE CONTROL JOINTS (T.C.J.) LOCATED AS PER T.T.M.A.C. RECOMMENDATIONS AND AS DETAILED AND INDICATED ON PLANS, & AT ALL VERTICAL TO HORIZONTAL JUNCTURES & AT ALL CATCHMENT AREA DELINEATION, & AT ALL SLAB POUR JOINTS, AND ADDITIONALLY AT MAX 4.5 M O.C. COORDINATE TILE CONTROL JOINTS WITH TILE MODULES, AND REVIEW LAYOUT WITH ARCHITECT PRIOR TO COMMENCING TILE WORK.

7. LOCATE STRUCTURAL CONTROL JOINTS IN DECK SLAB-ON-GRADES AREAS DIRECTLY BELOW ALL TILE CONTROL JOINTS, IF REQUIRED, SAW CUT CONTROL JOINT TO ALIGN WITH TILE MODULE.

8. SLOPE DECK TO DRAIN AT 2% MINIMUM, DO NOT EXCEED 5% SLOPE ANYWHERE ON DECK. ENSURE NO PONDING OF WATER.

9. ALL LAYOUT DIMENSIONS ARE TO SURFACE OF TILE FINISH. LOCATE CONCRETE SUBSTRATE ACCORDINGLY.

10. THE CHANGE ROOM FLOORS AT PERIMETER ARE DESIGNATED 0. ADVISE CONSULTANT OF ANY DISCREPANCIES PRIOR TO COMMENCING WORK.

11. SUPPLIER TO PROVIDE SHOP DRAWINGS SIGNED AND SEALED BY REGISTERED PROFESSIONAL FOR ALL GUARDS AND HANDRAILS.

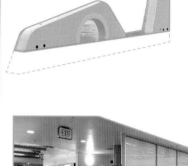

CLEAR SCRATCH RESISTANT LEXAN CIRCLES, POLISH ALL SIDES, BACK PAINT GRAPHIC, MOUNT WITH CONCELED FASTENERS OR ADHESIVE

CHANGE ROOM

NOTE:
REFER TO ELEVATIONS FOR LOCATIONS AND TEXT

TYPICAL SIGNAGE MOUNTING NTS — UNITS ARE MILLIMETRES

4 TYPICAL INTERIOR SIGNAGE
1/4" = 1'0"

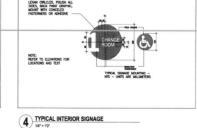

5 PRIVACY DETAILS
1/4" = 1'0"

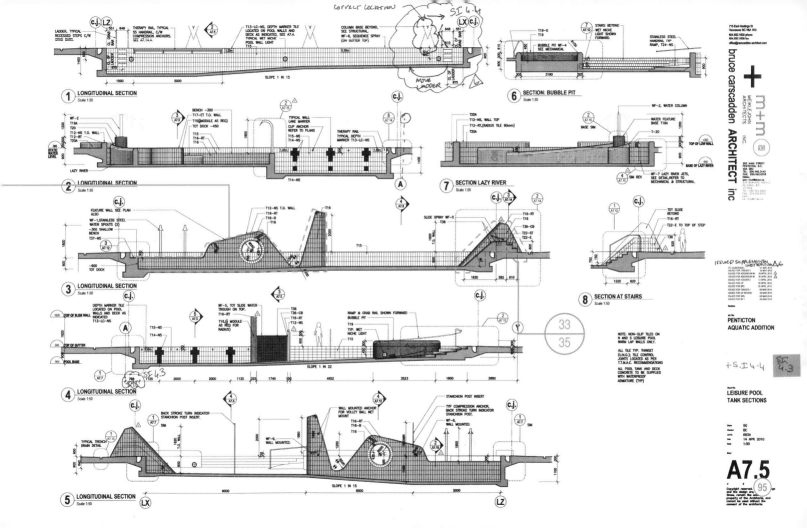

PRIVATE RESIDENCE

CLIENT	Private Client
DESIGN TEAM	Bruce Carscadden Architect, CY Loh & Associates, Cobalt Engineering, The MMM Group, Spratt Emmanuel Engineering, Catherine Macdonald
CONTRACTOR	G Wilson Construction

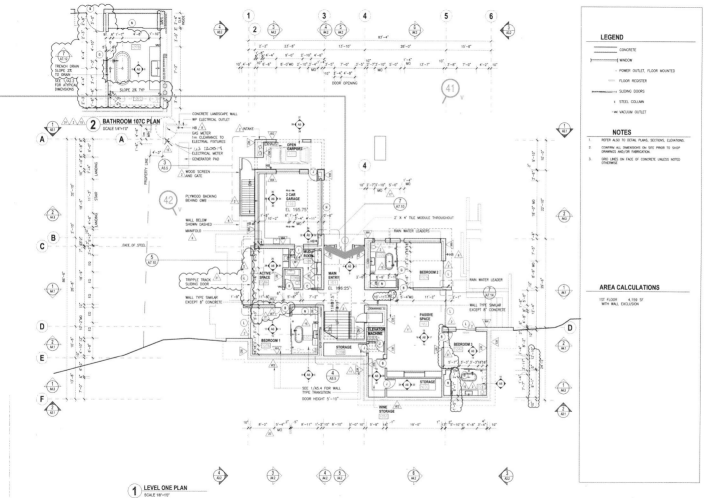

715 East Hastings Street
Vancouver BC V6A 1R3
604.633.1830 phone
604.633.1809 fax
office@carscadden-architect.com

bruce carscadden ARCHITECT inc

LEGEND

	CONCRETE
	WINDOW
•	POWER OUTLET, FLOOR MOUNTED
	FLOOR REGISTER
	SLIDING DOORS
⊥	STEEL COLUMN
∘vc	VACUUM OUTLET

NOTES

1. REFER ALSO TO DETAIL PLANS, SECTIONS, ELEVATIONS.
2. CONFIRM ALL DIMENSIONS ON SITE PRIOR TO SHOP DRAWINGS AND/OR FABRICATION.
3. GRID LINES ON FACE OF CONCRETE UNLESS NOTED OTHERWISE

AREA CALCULATIONS

1ST FLOOR   4,159 SF
WITH WALL EXCLUSION

1ST FLOOR PLAN

Drawn   ---
Checked ---
Job No   0629
Date   26 OCT 2007
Scale   1/8" = 1'

A2.2

BATHROOM 107C PLAN
SCALE 1/4"=1'0"

LEVEL ONE PLAN
SCALE 1/8"=1'0"

2 CAR GARAGE
EL 195.75'

OPEN CARPORT

MUD ROOM

MAIN ENTRY
EL 196.25'

ACTIVE SPACE

BEDROOM 1

BEDROOM 2

BEDROOM 3

PASSIVE SPACE

ELEVATOR MACHINE

STORAGE

STORAGE

WINE STORAGE

TRENCH DRAIN
SLOPE 2% TO DRAIN
SEE 1/A2.2 FOR ATYPICAL DIMENSIONS

SLOPE 2% TYP

CONCRETE LANDSCAPE WALL
WP ELECTRICAL OUTLET
GAS METER
1m CLEARANCE TO ELECTRICAL FIXTURES
ELECTRICAL METER
GENERATOR PAD
WOOD SCREEN AND GATE

PLYWOOD BACKING BEHIND GWB

WALL BELOW SHOWN DASHED

MANIFOLD

TRIPLE TRACK SLIDING DOOR

WALL TYPE SIMILAR EXCEPT 8" CONCRETE

FACE OF STEEL

2' X 4' TILE MODULE THROUGHOUT

RAIN WATER LEADERS

RAIN WATER LEADER

WALL TYPE SIMILAR EXCEPT 8" CONCRETE

SEE 1/A5.4 FOR WALL TYPE TRANSITION
DOOR HEIGHT 5'-10"

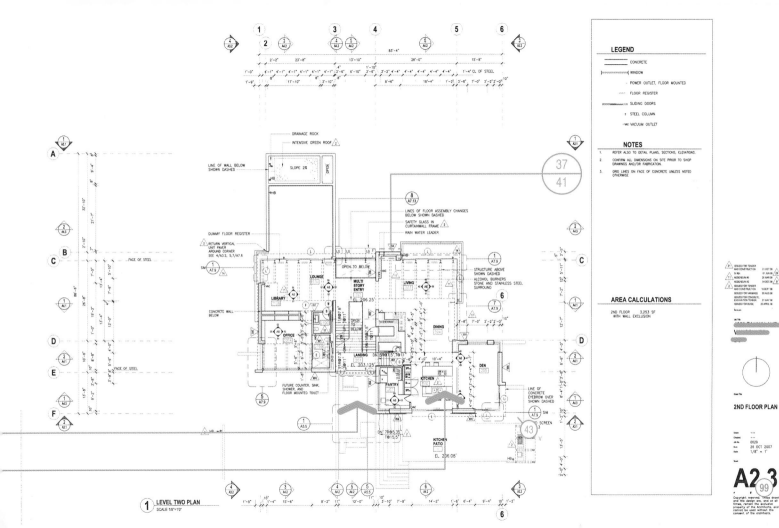

LEGEND

- CONCRETE
- WINDOW
- POWER OUTLET, FLOOR MOUNTED
- FLOOR REGISTER
- SLIDING DOORS
- STEEL COLUMN
- VAC VACUUM OUTLET

NOTES

1. REFER ALSO TO DETAIL PLANS, SECTIONS, ELEVATIONS.
2. CONFIRM ALL DIMENSIONS ON SITE PRIOR TO SHOP DRAWINGS AND/OR FABRICATION.
3. GRID LINES ON FACE OF CONCRETE UNLESS NOTED OTHERWISE

AREA CALCULATIONS

2ND FLOOR   3,253 SF
WITH WALL EXCLUSION

2ND FLOOR PLAN

Drawn   --
Checked   --
Job No.   0829
Size   26 OCT 2007
Scale   1/8" = 1'

A2.3

99

LEVEL TWO PLAN
SCALE 1/8"=1'0"

DRAINAGE ROCK
INTENSIVE GREEN ROOF
LINE OF WALL BELOW SHOWN DASHED
SLOPE 2%   OPEN
DUMMY FLOOR REGISTER
RETURN VERTICAL UNIT PAVER AROUND CORNER SEE 4/A3.2, 5,7/A7.6
FACE OF STEEL
CONCRETE WALL BELOW
FUTURE COUNTER, SINK, SHOWER, AND FLOOR MOUNTED TOILET

OPEN TO BELOW
LINES OF FLOOR ASSEMBLY CHANGES BELOW SHOWN DASHED
SAFETY GLASS IN CURTAINWALL FRAME
RAIN WATER LEADER
STRUCTURE ABOVE SHOWN DASHED
ALCOHOL BURNERS STONE AND STAINLESS STEEL SURROUND

LOUNGE
MULTI STORY ENTRY
EL 206.25'
LIBRARY
OFFICE
LIVING
DINING
LANDING
EL 203.125'
KITCHEN
PANTRY
DEN
LINE OF CONCRETE EYEBROW OVER SHOWN DASHED
KITCHEN PATIO
EL 206.08'

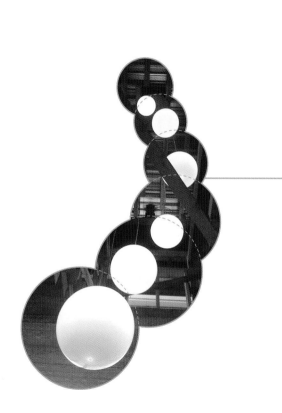

39
42

40
42

38
41

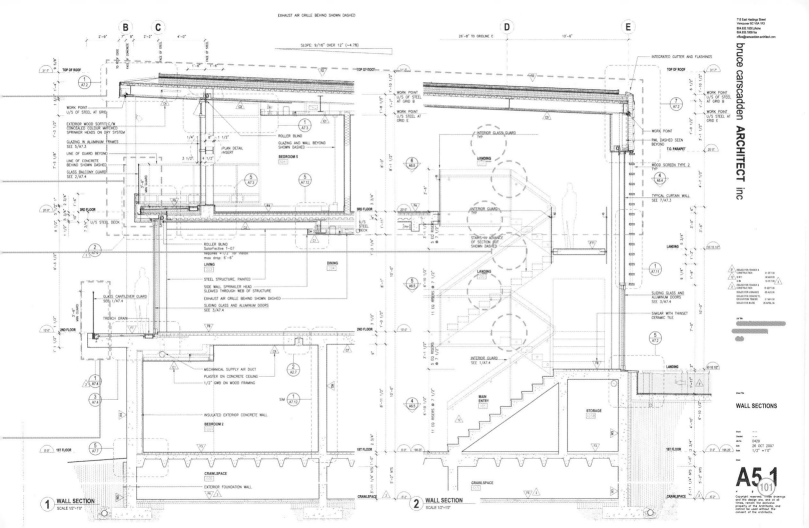

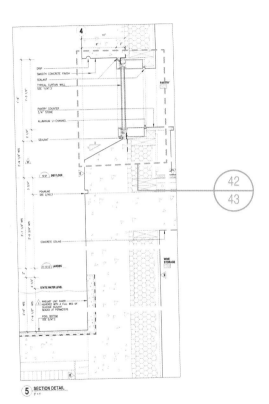

DRIP
SMOOTH CONCRETE FINISH
SEALANT
TYPICAL CURTAIN WALL
SEE 1/A1.3

PANTRY

PANTRY COUNTER
3/4" STONE
ALUMINUM U-CHANNEL

SEALANT

2ND FLOOR

POURLINE
SEE 2/40.3

CONCRETE CEILING

WINE
STORAGE

LANDING

STATIC WATER LEVEL

PRECAST UNIT PAVER
ADHERED WITH A FULL BED OF
SILICONE SEALANT
SEALED AT PERIMETERS
POOL BOTTOM
SEE 6/A7.3

5 **SECTION DETAIL**
3" = 1'

42
43

2 **SECTION AND RCP DETAIL**
SCALE 1 1/2"=1'-0"

JUNCTION BOX
(HVAC CADDIE)

PAINTED TO MATCH
CEILING HI BOARDING

PLASTER HI BEARDING
DOWN DOUBLE
PART BLOCKED AT
TO MATCH

RECESSED SIDEWALK "C"

COMMERCIAL SLED CUT AT
FLUSH WITH CONCRETE
CEILING

REFLECTED CEILING PLAN

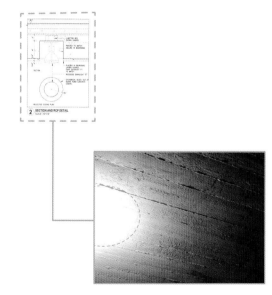

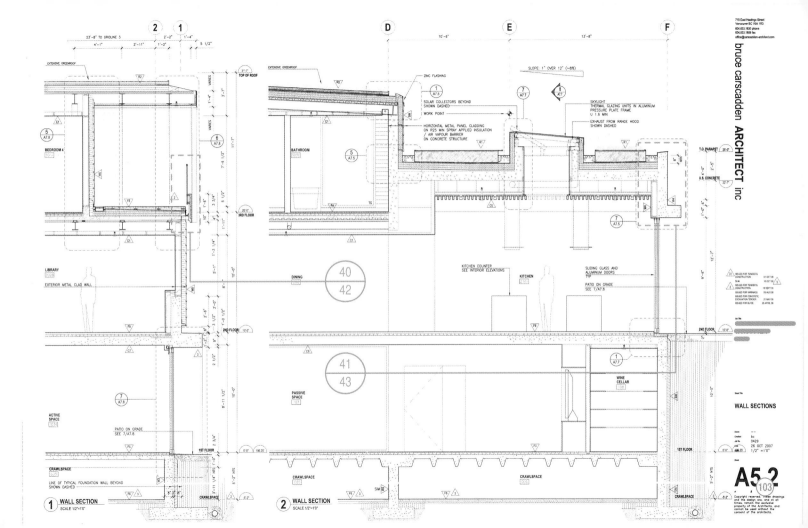

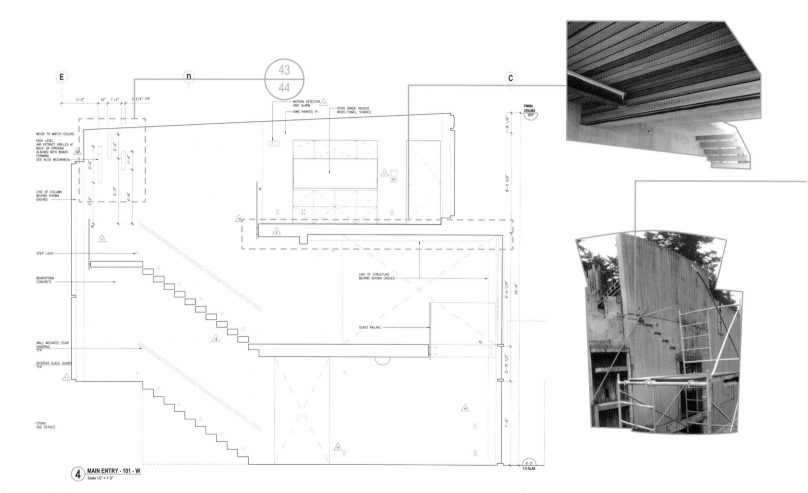

E   D   C

43
44

3'-2" 10" 1'-2" 3 3/4" TYP

MOTION DETECTOR
AND ALARM

STAIN GRADE VENEER
WOOD PANEL, STAINED

GWB PAINTED P1

FINISH
CEILING
28'4"

WOOD TO MATCH CEILING

HIGH LEVEL
AIR EXTRACT GRILLES AT
BACK OF OPENING
ALIGNED WITH BOARD
FORMING
SEE ALSO MECHANICAL

LINE OF COLUMN
BEHIND SHOWN
DASHED

STEP LIGHT

BOARDFORM
CONCRETE

LINE OF STRUCTURE
BEHIND SHOWN DASHED

WALL MOUNTED STAIR
HANDRAIL
TYP

GLASS RAILING

INTERIOR GLASS GUARD
TYP

STONE
SEE DETAILS

0'-0"
T.O SLAB

4 MAIN ENTRY - 101 - W
Scale 1/2" = 1'0"

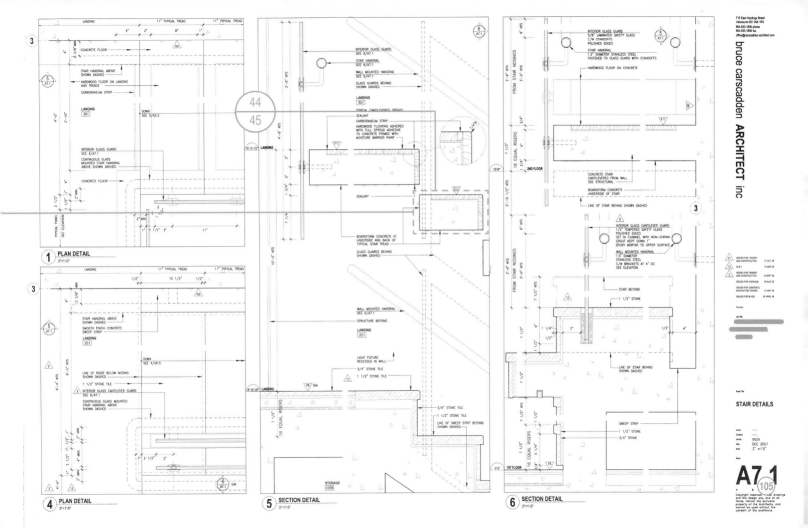

716 East Hastings Street
Vancouver BC V6A 1R3
604.633.1830 phone
604.633.1839 fax
office@carscadden-architect.com

bruce carscadden ARCHITECT inc

LANDING · 11" TYPICAL TREAD · 11" TYPICAL TREAD

3 —

CONCRETE FLOOR
3 3/4" MIN

STAIR HANDRAIL ABOVE
SHOWN DASHED

5 / A7.1
HARDWOOD FLOOR ON LANDING
AND TREADS

CARBORANEUM STRIP

LANDING
301

DOWN
SEE 5/A5.5

INTERIOR GLASS GUARD
SEE 6/A7.1

CONTINUOUS GLASS
MOUNTED STAIR HANDRAIL
ABOVE SHOWN DASHED

CONCRETE FLOOR

2 1/2"
2" MIN
2" MIN
1" 1/2" 3" 11"
TYPICAL PANEL,
SEE ELEVATION

1 PLAN DETAIL
3"=1'-0"

LANDING · 11" TYPICAL TREAD · 11" TYPICAL TREAD

3 —

STAIR HANDRAIL ABOVE
SHOWN DASHED

5 / A7.1
SMOOTH FINISH CONCRETE
SWEEP STRIP

LANDING
201

DOWN
SEE 4/A5.5

LINE OF RISER BELOW NOSING
SHOWN DASHED

1 1/2" STONE TILE

INTERIOR GLASS CANTILEVER GUARD
SEE 6/A7.1

CONTINUOUS GLASS MOUNTED
STAIR HANDRAIL ABOVE
SHOWN DASHED

1 1/2" 3"
1" 1/2" 3"
4" MAX
1" MIN

5 / A7.1 SIM

4 PLAN DETAIL
3"=1'-0"

INTERIOR GLASS GUARD
SEE 6/A7.1

STAIR HANDRAIL
SEE 6/A7.1

WALL MOUNTED HANDRAIL
SEE 6/A7.1

GLASS GUARDS BEHIND
SHOWN DASHED

LANDING
301

TYPICAL CANTILEVERED TREADS

SEALANT

CARBORANEUM STRIP
HARDWOOD FLOORING ADHERED
WITH FULL SPREAD ADHESIVE
TO CONCRETE PRIMED WITH
MOISTURE BARRIER PAINT

SEALANT

BOARDFORM CONCRETE AT
UNDERSIDE AND BACK OF
TYPICAL STAIR TREAD

GLASS GUARDS BEHIND
SHOWN DASHED

WALL MOUNTED HANDRAIL
SEE 6/A7.1

STRUCTURE BEYOND

LANDING
201

LIGHT FIXTURE
RECESSED IN WALL

3/4" STONE TILE

1 1/2" STONE TILE

3/4" STONE TILE

1 1/2" STONE TILE

LINE OF SWEEP STRIP BEYOND
SHOWN DASHED

16 EQUAL RISERS
7 1/2"

STORAGE
1058

5 SECTION DETAIL
3"=1'-0"

INTERIOR GLASS GUARD
5/8" LAMINATED SAFETY GLASS
C/W STANDOFFS
POLISHED EDGES

STAIR HANDRAIL
1.5" DIAMETER STAINLESS STEEL
FASTENED TO GLASS GUARD WITH STANDOFFS

HARDWOOD FLOOR ON CONCRETE

FROM STAIR NOSINGS

16 EQUAL RISERS
7 1/2"

2ND FLOOR

CONCRETE STAIR
CANTILEVERED FROM WALL
SEE STRUCTURAL

BOARDFORM CONCRETE
UNDERSIDE OF STAIR

LINE OF STAIR BEHIND SHOWN DASHED

3

INTERIOR GLASS CANTILEVER GUARD
1/2" TEMPERED SAFETY GLASS
POLISHED EDGES
SET IN CHANNEL WITH NON-SHRINK
GROUT KEPT DOWN 1"
EPOXY MORTAR TO UPPER SURFACE

WALL MOUNTED HANDRAIL
1.5" DIAMETER
STAINLESS STEEL
C/W BRACKETS AT 4" OC
SEE ELEVATION

STAIR BEYOND

1 1/2" STONE

FROM STAIR NOSINGS

16 EQUAL RISERS
7 1/2"

LINE OF STAIR BEHIND
SHOWN DASHED

SWEEP STRIP

1 1/2" STONE

3/4" STONE

16 EQUAL RISERS
7 1/2"

1ST FLOOR

6 SECTION DETAIL
3"=1'-0"

STAIR DETAILS

Drawn: --
Checked: --
Job No: 0629
Date: DEC 2007
Scale: 3" =1'-0"

A7.1

(105)

ON THRIFT

Bruce Carscadden Architect is a small design studio based in Vancouver, Canada. In nearly a decade of practice, our firm has designed and executed numerous building types for a variety of clients. Current work is typically public in nature, with an emphasis on community recreation projects in the Lower Mainland and Interior of British Columbia.

Always, we approach our work with the minimum solution as the constraint, seeking to amplify it without excess complication so that the inflection is inherent and empathetic. Our romantic ideal is the prairie farmer whose thrift and curiosity produce work that is direct in its assembly and continually refined through examination and application. The result for the farmer is an improved tool. For us it is a potential for delight that belies the familiar material origins of a space, and an economy that yields luxury in spite of itself.

Central to this inquiry is an understanding of assembly - the assembly of architecture, of course, but also of the assembly of documents and other instruments of architecture's agency. With that in mind, this document is structured in the spirit of that moment in a building's life most compelling to us: the translation from drawing (speculation) to material (actual). Photographs and drawings lay bare the chaotic reality of making, and while the analogy to a set of contract documents is obvious, it is not superficial. Both require examination in order to fully understand the nature of a project - projects that taken together have the capacity to describe the culture of the studio as well as our attempts to understand questions posited by the constraints of scale, site, and schedule.

We pursue an architecture that is occasionally messy in its creation, but hopefully complex and robust in its result. It is never perfect, so we continue to practice.

With thanks to our clients and collaborators, without whom we would have been better off being dentists and none of this would have been possible:

Grandview Elementary Outdoor Classroom
Pilley Rear Yard Infill House
Athans Aquatic Centre
Kimberly Aquatics
Langley Arena Seating
Revelstoke Aquatic Centre Feasibility Study
UBC Tectonics
Langley Box Seating
Williams Lake Aquatic Centre Feasibility Study (with PERC)
Kokanees Gymnasium
Castlegar Community Complex Feasibility Study
1300 Marine North Van
District 69 Arena Study (with PERC)
Castlegar Weights Room Addition
Louis Brier Hospital
4487 West 15th
West Vancouver Ice Ramp
65 Water Street
#140 943 West Broadway
West Vancouver Arena Upgrades
UBC School of Architecture Millwork
8130 Winston Burnaby
AIBC Education Centre
Langley Civic Centre Accessibility
Powell River Recreation Master Plan (with PERC)
Zima Pool (with FSC Architects & Engineers)
Renfrew Community Centre Pool Upgrades
Powell River Ice Slab Replacement
Kimberley Outdoor Pool
James Residence
33 Water Street
Wolfe Avenue Garage
Powell River Referendum (with PERC)
55 Kingsway

New Leaf Editions
55 Water Street Suites
Powell River Library Study (with PERC)
Nelson and District Recreation Project
Kimberley Referendum (with PERC)
Twenty Four Tenant Improvement
Chilliwack Arts Facility Feasibility Study
West Bank Recreation Centre Feasibility Study
943 West Broadway
UBC Crane Resource Centre
1936 Parker Street Garage
Burnaby Rinks Upgrades
de Leandro Restaurant
UBC Interfaith Centre
Salt Spring Island Residence
1944 Parker Street Garage
Nicomekl Park Skateboard Park Study
Similkameen Recreation Centre Study (with PERC)
1867 West 4th Avenue
Powell River Aquatic Centre Upgrades
Sandman Hotel-Penticton
Smithers-Bulkley Valley Pool Study (with PERC)
Bulkley Valley Hot Pool Renovation
Modernchild Tenant Improvement
Princeton and District Arena
580 Granville Street
1701 Powell Street Cafe
Oliver Aquatic Centre Feasibility Study (with PERC)
1014 Homer Street
18 West Hastings Street Heritage Restoration + MicroLofts
UBC Cunningham 282 + 284 Lab Upgrades
Creston Aquatic Centre Feasibility Study (with PERC)
Nelson Square Renovations
District of Kent Aquatic Centre Feasibility Study (with PERC)
Winfield Recreation Centre Master Plan (with PERC)
Eileen Daily Pool Reception Desk
Burnaby Arena Facilities & Services Review
Castlegar Arena Change Rooms Study
West Coast Recreation Centre Study
Cheam Centre Feasbility Study

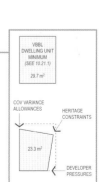

VBBL
DWELLING UNIT
MINIMUM
(SEE 10.21.1)

29.7 m²

COV VARIANCE
ALLOWANCES

HERITAGE
CONSTRAINTS

23.3 m²

DEVELOPER
PRESSURES

Mel Edwards Centre
UBC Library Processing Centre
UBC Brock Hall Renovations
1570 Kootenay Street
Canada Games Pool Waterslide
Golden Aquatic Centre Feasibility Study (with PERC)
North Vancouver Park Facility Study (with PERC)
Cheam Phase 2 Community Centre
The Noodle Box Tenant Improvements
Castlegar Change Room Upgrades
Kiwanis Outdoor Pool Review
1745 West 4th Avenue
Kelowna YMCA/YWCA Feasibility Study
Lord Strathcona Elementary Library Feasibility Study
Terrace Arena Expansion
Swalwell Park Washrooms
Nelson Square Lobbies
Travis Residence
UBC Cunningham 382 + 384 Lab Upgrades
Winfield Arena Mechanical Upgrades Study
George Preston Recreation Centre
Abbotsford Recreation Centre
Nelson Square Language School
4850 Fannin Avenue
Surrey Parks Strategic Plan (with PERC)
Chilliwack Paramount Theatre Study
WC Blair Centre Study (with PERC)
Princeton Public Library
Terrace Arena Interior Design
Nelson Square Residential Lobbies
808 Nelson Square-Suite 1302
Hazelton- Skeena Ice Arena Study
157 Alexander Street
Lake Country Fire Hall Study
Osoyoos Aquatic Centre Feasibility Study (with PERC)
Fort George Park Washroom and Picnic Shelter
Eastburn Community Centre Study (with HBBH)
Kensington Park Washrooms
Robert Burnaby Park Washrooms
65 Water Street Event Space

Chilliwack City Hall Addition Study
Eileen Dailly-First Aid Room
1014 Homer Street
Homedelight Tenant Improvement
Swalwell Park Pavilion
Campbell River Events Centre Study
LSI Tenant Improvement
Renfrew Pool Change Room Study
250 Willingdon Recreation Centre Study (with PERC)
Kerrisdale Professional Building
Brandon YMCA Aquatic Centre (with MCM Architects)
Winfield Arena Dressing Room Addition
Princeton Aquatic Centre Study (with PERC)
UBC Cunningham Basement Labs
Invermere Civic Centre Study
Nelson Square
715 East Hastings Street
Renfrew Change Rooms
Castlegar Arena Review
Eileen Daily Pool Review
Princeton Airport Terminal Building
Richmond Olympic Oval Aquatic Centre Study
1749 West 4th Avenue (The Boardroom)
Kent Aquatic Centre Feasiblity (with PERC)
Penticton Aquatic Expansion Study (with PERC)
Caulfield Liquor Store
Tom Forsyth Arena Study
Winfield Arena Phase 3 Feasibility Study (with PERC)
3438 Dundas Street
Coral Park Washrooms
Minoru Aquatic Centre Change Rooms
South Cariboo Aquatic Feasibility Study (with PERC)
1771 E Hastings
4866 Narvaez Drive
UBC Jack Bell Building Renovations
Princeton Town Hall Review
Broadmead Liquor Store
Jackson Avenue Green Roof
Steveston Community Centre Study
70 Eight Street New West TI

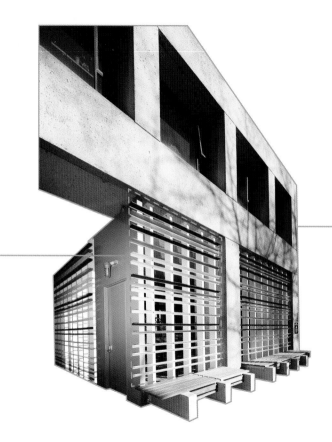

Rutland Arena West Slab Replacement
Smithers Recreation Multiplex Study (with PERC)
Squamish Liquor Store
Bonsor Envelope Upgrades
Kelowna YMCA Gym Addition Study
207 W Hastings Street
Bella Coola Aquatic Centre Feasibility Study (with PERC)
Minoru Change Rooms Phase 2
Cunningham Building Room 180A Split
Ladner Leisure Centre Feasibility Study
Amenity Building at Maffeo-Sutton Park
Vanderhoof Recreation Feasiblity Study (with PERC)
Castlegar Community Complex-Feasiblity Study 2010
Como Lake Liquor Store
Polson Park Pavilion
UBC Wesbrook Lab
Penticton Aquatic Centre Expansion
Sidney Liquor Store
Port Metro-Richmond Seismic Upgrades
Relish Tenant Improvement
Homer Street Noodle Box TI
UBC TREK Bike Shelters
Cloverdale Liquor Store
Good Shephard Church Renovations
Fireworks Design Tenant Improvements
Richmond Kawaki Site Study
Princeton Town Hall Phase 2
Winfield Arena Office Upgrades
Lake Country Municipal Hall Study
Ambleside Park Field House Renovations
UBC ICICS Building Renovations
Wreck Beach Public Washrooms
White Rock Public Washrooms
Kent Street Activity Centre Upgrades
Amarcord Restaurant TI
Steveston Community Centre Net Shed Upgrades
James Cowan Theatre Restrooms
Hay River Recreation Centre Study (with PERC)

AWARDS

BCRPA PROVINCIAL AWARDS PARKS AND OPEN SPACES AWARD (2011)
Swalwell Park

LIEUTENANT GOVERNOR OF BRITISH COLUMBIA AWARDS FOR ARCHITECTURE MEDAL (2009)
Swalwell Park, Kensington Park, and Robert Burnaby Park Washrooms

MASONRY INSTITUTE OF BRITISH COLUMBIA AWARD OF EXCELLENCE (2009)
Swalwell Park and Kensington Park Washrooms

CREATIVE ROOM GINGERBREAD COMPETITION
Second Prize for the Zen House

TIME MAGAZINE PERSON OF THE YEAR (2006)
Awarded for having, for better or worse, most influenced events in the preceding year

ENVIRONMENTAL STEWARDSHIP DESIGN AWARD (2001)
Grandview Elementary Outdoor Classroom

ATHLETIC BUSINESS FACILITY OF MERIT AWARD (2000)
Walnut Grove Aquatic Centre

AIA WESTERN INTL DESIGN AWARDS PROGRAM AWARD OF MERIT IN ARCHITECTURE (2000)
Renfrew Branch Library

LIEUTENANT GOVERNOR OF BRITISH COLUMBIA AWARDS FOR ARCHITECTURE MEDAL (2000)
Walnut Grove Aquatic Centre

CITY OF VANCOUVER HERITAGE AWARD (1999)
Architectural Institute of British Columbia Offices

INTERIOR DESIGN INSTITUTE OF BRITISH COLUMBIA AWARD (1998)
Architectural Institute of British Columbia Offices

RAIC GOVERNOR GENERAL'S AWARDS FOR ARCHITECTURE (1997)
Renfrew Branch Library

BRITISH COLUMBIA LIBRARIAN ASSOCIATION AWARD (1995)
Renfrew Branch Library

LIEUTENANT GOVERNOR OF BRITISH COLUMBIA AWARDS FOR ARCHITECTURE (1995)
Eileen Daily Leisure Pool & Fitness Centre

BRITISH COLUMBIA STEEL DESIGN AWARD (1993)
Eileen Daily Leisure Pool & Fitness Centre

RAIC GOVERNOR GENERAL'S AWARDS FOR ARCHITECTURE (1992)
Rogers Elementary School

CANADIAN ARCHITECT AWARD OF EXCELLENCE (1989)
Rogers Elementary School

*List includes projects while Project Architect or Partner with Roger Hughes + Partners Architects
(1998), Roger Hughes Architects (1996), and Hughes Baldwin Architects (1988-1995).*

CB INTERN ARCHITECT

INTERN ARCHITECT JR

IRM ASSOCIATE

MH ARCHITECT

KW ADMINISTRATION